WOULD YOU RATHER?...

EXTRA EXTREMELY EXTREME*

* Extremity Not Guaranteed

Over 1,500 Positively Preposterous Dilemmas to Ponder

Justin Heimberg & David Gomberg

Published by Seven Footer Press
276 Fifth Ave, Suite 301
New York, NY 10001

First Printing, August 2009
10 9 8 7 6 5 4 3 2
© Copyright Justin Heimberg and David Gomberg, 2009
All Rights Reserved

Cover Design by Junko Miyakoshi and Thomas Schirtz
Design by Thomas Schirtz

ISBN 978-1-934734-07-0

www.sevenfooterpress.com

TAKING
WOULD YOU RATHER...? TO THE EXTREME...
TO THE EXTREME!

"Extreme" is a relative term. There was a time when a simple tattoo was considered extreme; when a nose-piercing unquestionably pushed the boundaries of social decorum. But these days, one hardly blinks an eye if a man walks the streets with a tortoise chained to his bare testicles. We might shrug an "eh" if a motocross star does nine flips while farting the tune to the *Love Boat* theme.

We as a culture, assisted by the Internet, have defined deviance downward with an ever-accelerating velocity.

As a result, we've made it harder and harder to appear extreme. And so it becomes more and more difficult for us to serve up *Would You Rather...?* questions that shock, surprise, offend, or confuse. But, hey, we can still try.

Back in the day, we considered it extreme when our manuscript tallied the word count for "balls" at 12. But, rest assured, such a measly dozen testicle references does not meet modern day requirements for extreme. We've upped the ante. And years ago, our feeble minds thought over 200 absolutely absurd dilemmas was a more than adequately extreme amount of questions to offer as conversational fodder. But keeping up with the rates of informational inflation, we are now offering the balls[1]-out extreme 1,500+ dilemmas to ponder, laugh at, and discuss.

So challenge yourselves and your friends with questions that are extremely ridiculous, extremely absurd, extremely immature, and of course, extremely funny.

P.S. To the extreme.

---

[1] That makes two already.

HOW TO USE THIS BOOK

Sit around with a bunch of friends and read a question out loud. Discuss the advantages and drawbacks of each option before making a choice. Stretch, twist, and otherwise abuse your imagination to think of the multitude of ways the choice could affect you. The question is merely a springboard for your conversation.

Everybody must choose. As the Deity proclaims, YOU MUST CHOOSE! Once everyone has chosen, move on to the next question. It's that simple.

If you receive a question directed at females, and you are a male (or vice-versa), you can do one of several things: a) move on to another question, b) answer the question anyway, or c) freak out.

On occasion, we have provided some "things to consider" when making your decisions, but do not restrict yourself to those subjects when debating. There are no limits with this book, so go ahead and binge on the inappropriate and ridiculous, overindulge on the smorgasbord of absurdity, and stuff yourself silly.

WHAT PEOPLE ARE SAYING ABOUT
WOULD YOU RATHER...?
EXTRA EXTREMELY EXTREME!!!

"I don't have time to read it. I'm sorry."
— Joyce Carol Oates

"You'll have to talk to my publicist."
— Phillip Roth

"I'm sorry. Mr. Roth is not doing blurbs right now."
— Phillip Roth's Publicist

"I cannot help you."
— Maya Angelou

"My publicist handles these types of requests."
— Salman Rushdie

"We can't help you with that... I'm sorry to hear that it's
hard to get—... I am sympathetic...
Well then, maybe you should take a break."
— Salman Rushdie's Publicist

"So that's a large cheese and two Cokes, then?"
— Milt, Beach Pizza

"I'm sorry... What do you want me to do about it?...
You suck... No you suck... No, you suck!...
You suck infinity plus one."
— His Holiness, The Dalai Lama,
Author of *The Art of Happiness*

TABLE OF CONTENTS

CHAPTER ONE

SLIGHTLY EXTREME!

Oh yeah! That's right. These questions aren't for the faint of heart. No way, baby! Woohoooooo! Seniors!!!! However, nor do these questions exceed the daily recommended dosage of extremity (not extreme enough to drop the "E" and spell it X-treme, for instance). First things first. Start by challenging your friends with these quandaries ranging from the slightly extreme to the extremely slightly extreme to the slightly extremely slightly extreme!

Would you rather...

have granola boogers

OR

salt-and-pepper dandruff?

Things to consider: getting hungry on the trail, breakfast on the morning commute

Would you rather...

only be able to enter rooms via Kool-Aid man-style wall crashes

OR

only be able to exit rooms by jumping through a window as if fleeing a burning building?

Things to consider: cheery "Oh Yeah!"'s, panic-laden screams

Would you rather...

have orgasms as loud as a howler monkey

OR

orgasms as gushing as a Mentos dropped in Diet Coke?

YOU MUST CHOOSE!

Would you rather...

fall off a ladder and catch your eyelid on a nail

OR

slide down a banister of razor blades?

Would you rather...

have recess at your office

OR

have nap time?

Would you rather...

spend a minute in one of those glass cases of swirling money but have the dollar bills replaced with pieces of used toilet paper

OR

swim a lap in a pool of 65% urine/35% water?

YOU MUST CHOOSE!

Would you rather...

react like a dying Q*bert when you get frustrated and disappointed

OR

react like a dying Pac-Man when snubbed by a member
of the opposite sex?

Would you rather...

have a type of Tourette's Syndrome where you periodically
exclaim "Booyah!"

OR

have a facial tick to the rhythm of the opening bars of
"Eye of the Tiger"?

Things to consider: corporate presentations, your wedding ceremony

YOU MUST CHOOSE!

Would you rather...

sneeze a blast of shotgun pellets

OR

pee liquid nitrogen?

Things to consider: crime-fighting, potential for self-mutilation

Would you rather...

have sex with Rosie O'Donnell

OR

assume her physique?

Would you rather...

have to work on a computer from 1980

OR

use a cell phone from 1980?

YOU MUST CHOOSE!

Would you rather...

BE COMPELLED TO ENTER EVERY ROOM BY JUMPING INTO THE DOORWAY WITH AN IMAGINARY PISTOL LIKE THE STAR OF A '70S COP SHOW

OR

INVARIABLY MAKE YOUR ORGASM FACE INSTEAD OF SMILING WHEN BEING PHOTOGRAPHED?

Would you rather...

chisel off your nose

OR

your knee caps?

Would you rather...

have the heart rate of John McCain

OR

the blink rate of John McCain?

Would you rather...

have your child's babysitter be Johnny Knoxville

OR

Paula Abdul?

YOU MUST CHOOSE!

Would you rather...

be able to run a five minute mile but have an absurdly
effeminate stride

OR

be able to strut a seven minute mile?

Would you rather...

very slowly sandpaper the skin above your lip completely off

OR

take a BB gun, point it at your top right front tooth, and fire away?

Would you rather...

have a phone app where your phone blinks when someone is lying

OR

have an iDefibrillator app?

YOU MUST CHOOSE!

Would you rather...

dress like an 80 year-old **OR** walk like one?

have the face of an 80 year-old **OR** have the body of an 80 year-old?

have the face of an 80 year-old **OR** the face of a 2 year-old?

live in a world where we're able to iron our skin wrinkles like clothing **OR** where we continue to lose and gain teeth into adulthood?

age gracefully **OR** never age?

be 25 for your whole life **OR** not?

rust **OR** grow mold as you age?

SLIGHTLY EXTREME!

YOU MUST CHOOSE!

Would you rather...

have your social life restricted to comparing the absorbency of paper towels with middle-aged women like in those commercials

OR

have all your conversations have to in some way incorporate Simón Bolívar?

Things to consider: "That's interesting about your kid's soccer team. Perhaps they will play with the intensity of South American freedom fighter Simón Bolívar."

Would you rather...

only be able to drive on the wrong side of the road

OR

only be able to drive in reverse?

YOU MUST CHOOSE!

Would you rather...

BE STUCK ON A STALLED BUS WITH FORLORN ACCOUNTANTS

OR

NOSY PIRATES?

11

In order to defeat hostile enemies, would you rather MacGyver things into weapons from...

a 99 cent store **OR** a Bath & Body Works?

a farmer's market **OR** a Hallmark shop?

LensCrafters **OR** Burger King?

Things to consider: Explain your technique.

YOU MUST CHOOSE!

Would you rather...

insert a silent "d" in evdery wodrd tdhat dyou tydpe liked tdhis

OR

pronounce a "b" sound before every word you speak, as in "Buh-hi, buh-how, buh-you, buh-doing?"

Would you rather...

have lukewarm vision rays

OR

be able to silence your urinations when going in other people's bathrooms?

Would you rather name your child...

Adolph **OR** Fartsy?

Romulex **OR** Nips?

Destruction Personified **OR** 43?

YOU MUST CHOOSE!

Would you rather...

live in the world of present day rural Cambodia

OR

in the world of the Atari 2600's *Yar's Revenge*?

Would you rather...

have poppy-seeded skin

OR

have all of your social interaction carried out at the level of awkwardness and tedium of *Jeopardy* contestant exchanges with Alex Trebek?

Would you rather...

have your feces come out in a perfectly stacked pyramid of spheres (like cannon balls)

OR

brown bubbles that float in the air?

YOU MUST CHOOSE!

Would you rather...

have a 48 hour biological clock

OR

a 12 hour biological clock?

Would you rather...

have a literal beehive hairdo

OR

have literal muttonchops as sideburns?

Would you rather...

be able to handwrite any font at regular speed

OR

be able to flash a sincere smile on command for photographs?

YOU MUST CHOOSE!

Would you rather...

HAVE MAYONNAISE TEARS

OR

KOOL-AID SWEAT?

Would you rather read...

Pac-Man: The Novel

(Excerpt): Ever-chomping, Pac-Man fled, his mind a blur of dots and darkness. He was operating on instinct now, navigating the labyrinthine hell with a madness to match the situation. Blinky pursued, undead and pastel, the blank look in his eyes belying his thirst for death. And then, in an instant, it all changed. Night was day. Light was dark. For the gluttonous refugee had reached his engorged spheroid of power, and just like that, the chaser had become the chasee.

OR

Doom: The Novel

(Excerpt): He turned. He shot. The guy died. He turned again. He shot. Another guy died. He turned slightly. He shot. A guy died. He shot again. A guy died. He turned. He shot. He missed. He shot again. A guy died. He turned. He shot. A guy died. He was shot. He lost a portion of his life force. He shot. A guy died. He shot. A guy died. He moved forward. He turned. He shot. A guy died.

YOU MUST CHOOSE!

Would you rather...

HAVE AN 8 INCH WIDE INNIE BELLY-BUTTON

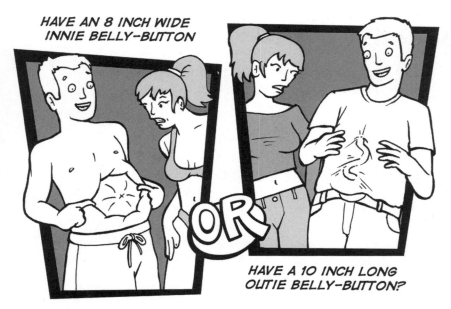

OR

HAVE A 10 INCH LONG OUTIE BELLY-BUTTON?

Would you rather...

cut off your arm using nothing but mini tweezers

OR

remove all of your teeth using a bottle opener?

Would you rather...

have a Norton virus checker for your body that would notify you about all viruses you get

OR

have a grammar check alert you when you speak incorrectly?

Would you rather...

have been college roommates with Gandhi

OR

Rube Goldberg?

Things to consider: late night BS sessions, elaborate phone answering devices, who was banging more chicks?

YOU MUST CHOOSE!

Would you rather...

have the letters on your keyboard randomly change places every day

OR

only be able to type with your thumbs?

Would you rather...

refer to yourself as "The Commandant"

OR

refer to yourself as "The 'Your Name'" like "The Donald" Trump?

YOU MUST CHOOSE!

Would you rather...

have Tyra Banks's forehead

OR

have Tyra Banks's brain?

Would you rather...

be a shapeshifter who can shift into the likeness of anyone named Darryl

OR

be tripolar (your moods swing wildly from joyful, to depressed, to being convinced you are an NBA referee in the middle of a game)?

YOU MUST CHOOSE!

AUTHORS' DEBATE

Would you rather...

fart a flamethrower's flame

Flame it Up by David Gomberg

Flamefarter. That's what your superhero name would be, along with the eponymous Marvel comic and mega-blockbuster they make based on your life. How exactly do you plan to fight crime by excreting dry ice? Fecal scented carbon dioxide is not a substantial impediment to villains and criminals. Not in the 21st century. And God, imagine the pain. Dry ice in its solid form is $-109.3\ °F$. Put simply, its enthalpy of sublimation (Hsub) at $-78.5\ °C$ ($-109.3\ °F$) is 571 kJ/kg (245 BTU/lb). Ouch!

YOU MUST CHOOSE!

OR defecate dry ice?

Ice Man by Justin Heimberg

Dumping dry ice will chap the sphincter, true, but farting flames isn't exactly Charmin-soft on the tussy. I think "Flamefarter" may be suffering from delusions of grandeur along with his third degree anus burns. A more logical comic book moniker for the one with the flaming anus is The Human Kiln, seeing that firing pottery via fart is the most utilitarian function I can think of for such a "talent." You'd have to buy crotchless pants or chaps since you'll be singeing your trousers every time a silent-but-wounding whisper of a soft flamefart ekes out. With the dry ice, your rectum will chap up after the first few BM's, and then you're just dealing with smoking stools. Not too shabby.

YOU MUST CHOOSE!

SLIGHTLY EXTREME!

EXTRA EXTREMELY EXTREME EXTRAS:

Would You Rather...? Presents 10 Things to Do at a Job Interview to Screw with the Interviewer

① At the top of your resume, print (in italics) song lyrics that inspire you, such as:

I would fight for you - I'd lie for you
Walk the wire for you - yeah I'd die for you
You know it's true.
Everything I do - I do it for you.
— Bryan Adams (from *Robin Hood, Prince of Thieves*)

② Smell your fingers periodically.

③ Quote Jesus a little too often.

④ Need a ride home.

⑤ Refer to yourself several times as a "grown-ass man", as in "I don't need micromanaging. I'm a grown-ass man."

⑥ Bring an "attorney" to your interview. Consult the attorney whenever you're asked a question, and have the attorney whisper to you before answering.

YOU MUST CHOOSE!

⑦ Wink frequently.

⑧ Bring a pocket dictionary. Every time the interviewer mentions a mildly sophisticated word, open the dictionary, look up the word, repeat the definition quietly, and then close the dictionary and answer the question normally.

⑨ List all of your references as "Deceased".

⑩ Listen attentively to the interviewer's explanation of the company. Then, with a deadpan expression, point to the appropriate body parts and say "Milk, milk, lemonade, 'round the corner, fudge is made." (Perfect opportunity to wink.)

For more material like this, check out the book MindF*cks by Justin Heimberg and David Gomberg and Google the short videos Do Unto Others.

YOU MUST CHOOSE!

C H A P T E R   T W O

EXTREMELY SEXUAL

Sex is a perfect example of an area where the boundaries of "extreme" expand every day. S&M is the new second base. Threesomes have given way to dodecasomes. A kiss goodnight on a first date? That's right, it's been replaced with a goodnight Cleveland Steamer on the first date. And so, we as cultural commentators, must "progress" with the times, offering up quandaries that play with the ever-expanding limits of sexual taboo.

Would you rather...

orgasm every 20 years

OR

orgasm every 20 yards?

Things to consider: the hundred yard dash, long hallways, playing football

Would you rather...

come home to find your parents reading your diary

OR

reading the *Kama Sutra*?

Would you rather...

have genitalia that whistle like a tea pot when you get turned on

OR

genitalia that emit a loud buzz and flashes a *Family Feud* "X" when you're turned off?

YOU MUST CHOOSE!

Would you rather have sex with...

Johnny Depp **OR** Brad Pitt?

50 Cent **OR** Dr. Drew?

Matthew Fox **OR** Jake Gyllenhaal?

Jimmy Kimmel **OR** Mitt Romney?

a first cousin of your choice **OR** John Madden?

Would you rather...

have sex with Padma Lakshmi

OR

get a five course *Top Chef* meal cooked to your specifications?

YOU MUST CHOOSE!

Would you rather have sex with...

Angelina Jolie **OR** Megan Fox?

Halle Berry **OR** Heidi Klum?

Reese Witherspoon **OR** Elisabeth Hasselbeck?

George Clooney **OR** Kirstie Alley at her heaviest/sloppiest?

Would you rather...

receive a Twitter tweet every time your partner has sexual thoughts about another person

OR

not?

YOU MUST CHOOSE!

Would you rather...

passionately make out with a heavy drooler

OR

give oral sex to a heavy farter?

Would you rather...

be unable to refrain from spastically "freaking" anyone you see over 70 years old

OR

upon saying goodbye, be unable to refrain from patting anyone under 14 on the butt with a friendly tap and a wink?

Would you rather...

get sexually aroused by the *NBC Nightly News* theme

OR

be turned on by dirty talk spoken in the style of a Cockney British orphan child?

YOU MUST CHOOSE!

Would you rather...

have your sexual fantasies edited for appropriate television viewing

OR

have the *Reading Rainbow* guy appear and tell you the moral at the end of every masturbation fantasy?

Things to consider: passionate kissing, implied intercourse

Would you rather have sex with...

Jessica Simpson if she gained 100 pounds **OR** Helen Mirren?

Jessica Alba and get herpes **OR** Meredith Viera and get a new X-box?

A limbless Adriana Lima **OR** Joy Behar?

Would you rather have sex with...

Brad Pitt if he gained 60 pounds all in the gut **OR** Jonah Hill?

a gap-toothed Matt Damon **OR** Chris Parnell?

Louie Anderson **OR** a racist-remark-spouting Tom Brady?

YOU MUST CHOOSE!

Would you rather...

have the sounds of your love-making uploaded everyday on iTunes

OR

have a video of you in the throes of masturbation posted on YouTube?

Would you rather...

have upside-down genitals

OR

have genitals rotated 90 degrees?

Would you rather...

have your wedding videographer be Joe Francis (creator of *Girls Gone Wild*)

OR

have your wedding ceremony officiated by Flavor Flav?

YOU MUST CHOOSE!

33

Would you rather...

have "innie" nipples

OR

inch-long curly nipples?

Would you rather...

have a sexual partner who has a lettuce fetish

OR

a foot-measuring device fetish?

Would you rather...

have sex with Cookie Monster

OR

Oscar the Grouch

Things to consider: CM's insatiable and feverish dining style, bad boys, stench

YOU MUST CHOOSE!

Would you rather have sex with...

Natalie Portman **OR** Mila Kunis?

Kate Hudson **OR** Anne Hathaway?

Hayden Panettiere **OR** Mandy Moore?

Christina Ricci **OR** Scarlett Johansson?

Dame Judi Dench **OR** Chyna?

Would you rather...

have sex on a sex swing

OR

in zero gravity?

YOU MUST CHOOSE!

Would you rather have sex with...

Javier Bardem **OR** Christian Bale?

Jon Stewart **OR** Stephen Colbert?

Adam Brody **OR** Michael Cera?

Nick Carter **OR** Aaron Carter?

a Teenage Mutant Ninja Turtle **OR** Mike Huckabee?

Would you rather...

be a teenager in the free love '60s

OR

in the '70s when air-brushed vans with beds and shag carpets were
totally acceptable?

YOU MUST CHOOSE!

Would you rather be forced to always have sex...

to the soundtrack of *High School Musical* **OR** festive Indian music?

in strobe light **OR** with NASCAR airing in the background?

in libraries **OR** in janitorial closets?

Would you rather have all of your sexual dreams directed by...

Jerry Bruckheimer **OR** Judd Apatow?

the Wachowski brothers **OR** the Coen brothers?

David Lynch **OR** Pixar?

YOU MUST CHOOSE!

Would you rather...
orgasm every time your cell phone rings

OR
have your cell phone ring every time you are about to orgasm?

Would you rather...
always have sex standing up

OR
without ever facing one another?

Would you rather...
(men read as "date someone with...")
have no vagina

OR
have 17 vaginas all over your body?

YOU MUST CHOOSE!

Would you rather...

have a partner have to pee in the middle of sex

OR

answer a text message in the middle of sex?

Would you rather...

relive your first kiss

OR

relive your first sexual experience?

Would you rather...

spank

OR

be spanked?

YOU MUST CHOOSE!

Would you rather...

HAVE AN INCREDIBLY ADHESIVE FACE

OR

A HIGHLY MAGNETIC SCROTUM?

Would you rather change your name to...

(women, read as "marry and take the name of")

Derrick Fingerblast

OR

Ronald Queefcloud?

Would you rather...

be able to blow visible kisses across a room

OR

be able to fart directionally with an accuracy of 40 feet?

YOU MUST CHOOSE!

Would you ever have sex...

in a dressing room stall at the mall?

in a car in a public parking lot?

in your parents' bed?

on an airplane?

in the windmill of a minigolf course at night 'cause you think no one is there but then someone comes out, and you quickly try to pretend you are playing golf, but you have no clubs and your pants are around your ankles, so you just look like some kind of mime performance art group and you get arrested and have to pay a fine and are banned from that Putt-Putt forever?

YOU MUST CHOOSE!

Would you rather...

have a three-way with Carrie Underwood and Clay Aiken **OR** Adam Lambert and Kelly Clarkson?

Sarah Palin and John McCain **OR** Barack Obama and Hillary Clinton?

Serena Williams and Venus Williams **OR** Petra Nemcová and Urkel (in character)?

Would you rather...

have a threesome with Heidi and Spencer

OR

a brawl with Heidi and Spencer?

YOU MUST CHOOSE!

Would you...

make an agreement with your partner to allow each other three celebrities with whom infidelity would be permitted? If so, who would each of you pick?

Would you rather...

have sex with all celebrities whose last names begin with L **OR** W?

G **OR** D?

C **OR** R?

Would you rather...

come home to find your partner cheating on you

OR

wake up in the middle of the night to find your partner online and masturbating to screen shots of Fozzie Bear?

YOU MUST CHOOSE!

Would you rather...

have feathered hair

OR

have feathered pubic hair?

Would you rather...

have sex with the man who voices AOL

OR

with the man who voices movie previews?

Would you rather...

receive the memories of anyone you sleep with

OR

not?

YOU MUST CHOOSE!

Would you rather have...

(women read as "have a partner with...")
a set of drill-bit like different penis heads

OR

a penis that can be adjusted and reconfigured like the Rubik's Snake?

Would you rather have sex with...

Amanda Bynes **OR** Hilary Duff?

Michelle Pfeiffer **OR** Heather Locklear?

Sarah Jessica Parker **OR** Meg Ryan?

Jessica Biel **OR** Cameron Diaz?

Perez Hilton **OR** Tim Gunn?

YOU MUST CHOOSE!

Would you rather have sex with...

The Rock **OR** Denzel Washington?

Bono **OR** Sting?

Ryan Gosling **OR** Jake Gyllenhaal?

Justin Timberlake **OR** Kanye West?

John Mayer **OR** Jack Johnson?

Would you rather...

know what it is like to physically experience sex
as the opposite gender

OR

know what it is like to emotionally experience love
as the opposite gender?

YOU MUST CHOOSE!

Would you rather...

have nipples that turn green and burst out of your clothing when you get angry

OR

have grappling hook nipples?

Would you rather...

have breast implants filled with birdseed

OR

breast implants filled with the stuff in rainsticks?

Would you rather...

have a total poker face when having an orgasm

OR

speak like an old radio crooner during sex?

YOU MUST CHOOSE!

AUTHORS' DEBATE

Would you rather...

your only porn be science books

Science Books – David Gomberg

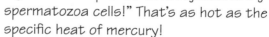

I'll take the vague shape of the body, organs exposed, over the history book masturbance of a sickly malnourished native Amazonian tribeswoman with diseased saggy breasts dripping to the ground, nipples scraping and tilling the soil. The circulatory system? Hot. Or maybe the pancreas is your thing. One last point: Don't forget that health and sex ed find their way into science books, too. So you can informatively grunt, "I'm gonna ram that labia majoris with the glans of the phallus until I ejaculate my

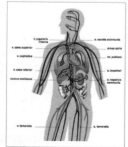

spermatozoa cells!" That's as hot as the specific heat of mercury!

YOU MUST CHOOSE!

OR history books?

History Books – Justin Heimberg

Like you haven't pleasured yourself to Harriet Tubman already? Givin' her the old "Underground Railroad." And Susan B "Doin' it" Anthony? She's got an ass that won't quit. Not until women's suffrage is achieved, at least. (By the way, can we change the word "suffrage" to mean something bad? It's confusing.) The point is that there are plenty of historic vixens to smack it to. The tomboy thing that Joan of Arc has going. The erotic mystique of Cleopatra, the eloquent dirty talk of Abigail Adams. It's true what they say:

Susan B. Anthony

Sometimes we have to look backward to spew forth.

EXTREMELY SEXUAL

YOU MUST CHOOSE!

EXTRA EXTREMELY EXTREME EXTRAS:

Facts That Sound For a Second Like They Might Be True But Aren't

A small amount of heroin is used in the manufacturing of Sunny Delight Citrus Drink.

Women originally wore makeup for warmth.

The reason Tom Selleck grew his mustache is because it helps with his allergies.

Soccer was invented on pirate ships as a means of cleaning the deck.

Water on the left side of the pool is always colder than water on the right side.

The Chinese government removes organs from Olympic gymnasts and wrestlers to make them lighter.

The back of a stamp has 70% of the daily requirement of riboflavin.

YOU MUST CHOOSE!

Statistically speaking, billiards is America's deadliest sport.

The people in pictures that come with wallets are prisoners whose services are not paid for, but rather mandated by law.

The letter "w" was added to the English language in 1954.

In any room of 20 people, there is a 50% chance that at least two people received the same birthday present last year.

Waffles have indentations on them because on Hanukah, the fleeing Jewish people did not have enough batter to make them to even thickness.

YOU MUST CHOOSE!

CHAPTER THREE

EXTREMELY PAINFUL
AND EXTREMELY FATAL

Feeling a wee bit masochistic, are we? It's ok. It's a part of human nature to have occasional thoughts of self-harm. Of course, the following thoughts are beyond the natural. Did someone say "extreme"?! No? Oh, I thought I heard something. My bad. Anyway, here are some cruel and unusual options to grimace to as you make your choice. And as always, you must choose. *To the extreme!!!!*

Would you rather...

use the "Rabbit" corkscrew to pluck out your left eyeball

OR

have your fingernails and toenails chiseled off one by one?

Would you rather...

have a pebble sewn into the bottom of your left foot

OR

have a sesame seed lodged uncomfortably and permanently between your front teeth?

Would you rather...

take a power drill up each nostril and then snort cayenne pepper

OR

have your testicles used as a pro boxer's speed bag for two minutes?

YOU MUST CHOOSE!

Would you rather...

die a quick death

OR

die an elaborate and drawn-out death by an overly complicated mechanism with a long speech by a James Bond-esque villain?

Would you rather...

be buried alive in a coffin full of fire ants

OR

be buried alive in a coffin with a wacky morning DJ show being piped in?

Would you rather...

have your lips belt-sanded off

OR

your jaw squeezed in a vice until it was dislocated?

YOU MUST CHOOSE!

57

Would you rather...

be murdered by Carrot Top who performs prop comedy with your dismembered body parts and organs

OR

be murdered by the author of *Family Circus* who offers barely amusing observations about everyday life as he butchers you?

Would you rather...

after you die, be pickled and displayed at the local bar

OR

be frozen in carbonate á la Han Solo and have your model mass-produced and sold as a coffee table at IKEA?

5TH GRADE SPECIAL

Would you rather...

get Indian-burned to death

OR

noogied to death?

YOU MUST CHOOSE!

Would you rather...

swallow and pass a shoehorn

OR

a Rubik's Cube?

Would you rather...

have your face repeatedly paddled for five minutes by ping pong world champions

OR

have somebody do the "got your nose" trick and really rip off your nose in a bloody mess?

Would you rather...

be strangled to death with black licorice

OR

be suffocated by basil leaves?

Things to consider: Novel idea: *The Herb Killer*, he killed leaving nothing but a pleasant scent.

YOU MUST CHOOSE!

Would you rather...

have two ice picks jammed in your ears and then smashed with a mallet

OR

have your arms folded behind your back and forced up until your shoulders popped out of their sockets?

Would you rather fight to the death...

Bambi **OR** Dumbo?

2,000 houseflies **OR** one donkey?

A rabid St. Bernard **OR** Milli Vanilli?

5,000 origami creations **OR** 100 pairs of high-tops?

A supervillain called "The Caddy" **OR** a supervillain called "The Receptionist"?

75 sloths **OR** 4,000 snails?

YOU MUST CHOOSE!

61

Would you rather...

take a sledgehammer to the back of both your ankles

OR

have your tongue whipped 500 times with a bamboo rod?

Would you rather...

be stoned to death with Koosh balls **OR** with hardboiled eggs?

by light bulbs **OR** cantaloupes?

by Randy Johnson **OR** by Randy Jackson?
Things to consider: Are you better off facing someone with good aim/speed?

Would you rather...

be clobbered to death with zucchini

OR

be suffocated to death with zucchini?

YOU MUST CHOOSE!

Would you rather...

take wire cutters and snip between your fingers centimeter by centimeter all the way to your wrist

OR

take some hedge clippers and clip your ears off?

Would you rather...

insert dozens of popcorn kernels way up into your sinus cavities and then hold your face over heat until the kernels popped

OR

place a lit M80 firecracker in your mouth and hold your breath until it explodes?

Would you rather...

get stuck on an elevator with gossipy seventh grade girls

OR

an Armenian businessman talking loudly on his cell phone?

YOU MUST CHOOSE!

Would you rather...

FIGHT 1 VICIOUS WEREWOLF

OR

8 BASHFUL VAMPIRES?

Would you rather...

get stuck on a desert island with a hot person who you can't have sex with

OR

a hideous person that wants to constantly have sex?

Would you rather...

be killed by a firing squad of badminton birdies

OR

be slapped to death by your entire neighborhood?

Would you rather...

be drawn and quartered

OR

be drawn and fifthed? Sixthed?

YOU MUST CHOOSE!

Would you rather...

sit on a fire hose for five minutes

OR

sit on an electric burner for one minute?

Would you rather...

have an electric tire pump shoot air into both your nostrils at full
speed until your nose explodes

OR

have a high-powered vacuum attached to your crotch until at least
something separated from your body?

Would you rather...

fight a creature with the body of a jaguar and the head
of a cow

OR

fight a creature with the body of a horse and the head
of Phyllis Diller?

YOU MUST CHOOSE!

Would you rather...

have your thumbs smashed by a hammer

OR

have a five inch screw slowly screwed into your navel?

Would you rather...

take ten clean shots in the chin from a boxer

OR

have your testicles neatly placed on a tee and then whacked by Tiger Woods?

Would you rather...

be rolling pinned to death

OR

beaten to death with spatulas?

YOU MUST CHOOSE!

Would you rather...

die by car accident

OR

via purple nurple?

Would you rather...

be attacked by 100 Monchichis

OR

1,000 Weebles?

Would you rather...

cut your own leg off

OR

cut off your significant other's?

YOU MUST CHOOSE!

Would you rather...

lie spread eagle and have a monster truck run over you right down the middle of your body

OR

be shaken to death in a giant version of Boggle?
Things to consider: imprints on your corpse

Would you rather...

die like a slug (be salted to death)

OR

be lemon-peppered to death? Paprika'ed to death?

Would you rather...

have all your skin peeled off with a carrot peeler

OR

have your arm veins pulled out of your skin by pliers?

YOU MUST CHOOSE!

PICK YOUR TRAUMA.

Would you rather...

be partially molested by a Yeti (groping, improper talk)

OR

be fully molested by Snuggles the Fabric Softener Bear?

Would you rather...

be fatally trampled by a diagonal jumping Q*bert

OR

killed by a Donkey Kong–like ape rolling barrels at you?

Would you rather...

eat thirty jalapeños with no water

OR

use poison ivy to blow your nose?

YOU MUST CHOOSE!

Would you rather...

be fully awake with no painkillers during a liver transplant

OR

during the removal of a testicle?

Would you rather...

get gored by a bull

OR

bullied by a Gore?

Would you rather...

get a paper cut between each of your toes and then step into a bucket of salt

OR

shave with a butcher's knife and then use vinegar aftershave?

YOU MUST CHOOSE!

DEATH BY CHEF

Would you rather...

be roasted on a spit until your meat fell off the bone **OR** be toasted to death?

be butterflied and stuffed with crabmeat and sautéed **OR** be blended and consumed as a smoothie?

be dehydrated to death **OR** garnished to death?

for ten minutes, dip your foot into a blender set on the lowest setting **OR** set on the highest setting?

Would you rather...

be caught in a hailstorm of thumbtacks

OR

a rainstorm of fire-crackers?

YOU MUST CHOOSE!

Would you rather...

set your foot on a tee and have Albert Pujols take a clean swing at it

OR

take a Johan Santana fastball to the small of the back?

Would you rather...

be dipped in liquid nitrogen and then pushed off a ten story building so you shattered upon impact

OR

be fly-swatted to death?

YOU MUST CHOOSE!

PERPETUAL FEELINGS

Would you rather...

perpetually experience déjà vu **OR** perpetually be about to remember the name of an obscure song but not quite have it?

perpetually have a "turtle" ebbing in and out of your butt **OR** perpetually feel like you do when your chair is about to fall backwards?

perpetually feel the awkwardness of when they sing "Happy Birthday" to you at a restaurant **OR** perpetually feel the lack of enthusiasm and insincerity that one of the singers feels?

YOU MUST CHOOSE!

WATER WARS

Would you rather fight to the death...

three manatees **OR** 300 flounder?

20,000 guppies **OR** one swordfish?

five beavers **OR** one retarded merman?

Would you rather...

be strapped to a table and have a drop of water repeatedly drip on your forehead

OR

be strapped to a table and have your eyes continuously pried open as you watch a one week marathon of *According to Jim*?

YOU MUST CHOOSE!

Would you rather...

be submerged into a deep fryer over and over until you died

OR

be microwaved to death?

Would you rather...

melon-ball your tonsils out

OR

punch yourself in the face until you knocked out all of your teeth?

Would you rather...

pull out all of your hair with your bare hands

OR

use a nutcracker on your testicles?

YOU MUST CHOOSE!

Would you rather...

have string tightened throughout your body turning you into a human sausage until the blocked blood flow kills you

OR

be stabbed to death by Capri Sun straws?

Would you rather...

wash your face with liquid nitrogen

OR

floss with razor wire?

YOU MUST CHOOSE!

AUTHORS' DEBATE

Would you rather fight to the death...

three 90 year-olds

90s Rule – Justin Heimberg

90 year-olds are brittle. Their old bones break and snap like balsa wood. Three year-olds are rubbery, resilient. They bounce back from things. Sure, they'll cry, but in their tantrum, they are that much more dangerous (and annoying.) It's their battle cry. 90 year-olds are most likely nearly blind. There's a decent chance you can turn them on each other by removing their bifocals and capitalizing on their senility. Three year-olds are right at crotch level, which is very dangerous. That's 18 tiny fists to the groin. I don't like those odds.

YOU MUST CHOOSE!

OR 9 three year-olds?

3rd *time's the charm* – David Gomberg

90 year-olds have hunched up a bit, but they are still roughly full—size. With the nine three year-olds, you can pretty much defend yourself with your legs. A couple of well-reasoned knees to the faces, and those three year-olds will be nursing bloody noses in the corner. 90 year-olds don't give up. They have nothing to lose. They'll scratch, claw, and sink their dentures into you. They'll fight until the last drop of blood drips from their almost empty tank. Three year-olds can be easily distracted. Hand them a Tickle Me Elmo and as they lose themselves in amusement, BAM! — elbow to the jaw.

YOU MUST CHOOSE!

EXTRA EXTREMELY EXTREME EXTRAS:
Terrible First Sentences for a Novel

Klarence liked his women like he liked his kickball pitches—slow and smooth.

Barney stood proudly in his lemon-peel pants.

She was all ligaments.

The pilgrim's orgy was a disaster.

Before going in, Larry put his underpants over his fist.

Elegar the Druid plunged his +5 Doom Broad Sword (transferring) into the barked neck of Lezzen the Orc Prince, Shelby the Bloated watching from the dark pools molting like there was no tomorrow.

Needledorf was his name; Needledorf, by coincidence, was also his game.

The joy in his heart spread like athlete's foot (spreads).

The sun set downward.

YOU MUST CHOOSE!

CHAPTER FOUR

FAIRLY EXTREME

This chapter is beyond slightly extreme, more out there than somewhat extreme! That's right, we're talking "Fairly Extreme!"

Would you rather...

have to sit in a baby-seat high chair at all restaurants

OR

have to use a sippy cup for all beverage consumption?

Things to consider: business lunches

Would you rather...

have the National Anthem changed to "Whip It"

OR

the Pledge of Allegiance changed to the lyrics of "Baby Got Back"?

Things to consider: Place your hand over your heart and try both

Would you rather...

have the pathetic "whah, whah, whah, whah" sound play whenever something bad happens to you

OR

have the joyful "Price is Right" music play when something good happens?

YOU MUST CHOOSE!

Would you rather...

the afterlife was a Staples office supply store

OR

an endless corporate retreat?

Would you rather...

have pubic hair eyelashes

OR

have no eyelashes?
Things to consider: mascara

Would you rather...

always look bruised as if beaten but feel no actual pain

OR

feel like you're bruised but look fine?

YOU MUST CHOOSE!

Would you rather...

have rosemary facial hair

OR

compulsively greet people with a "healing" palm to the forehead and accompanying praise to the Lord?

Would you rather...

have a wedding in the tone of a screwball comedy

OR

a Kung Fu movie?

Things to consider: ice sculptures, bouquet battles, ninja veils

YOU MUST CHOOSE!

Which coffee invention would you rather have?

a coffee straw that cools coffee enough that you don't burn your mouth

OR

a sugar dispenser that dispenses an exact spoonful of sugar with each tap?

Would you rather eat all meals...

with chopsticks **OR** with a spork?

with your hands **OR** by being fed by other people?

with Alf **OR** with Lauren Conrad?

YOU MUST CHOOSE!

Would you rather...

BE A SIAMESE TWIN CONNECTED AT THE SOLES OF YOUR FEET

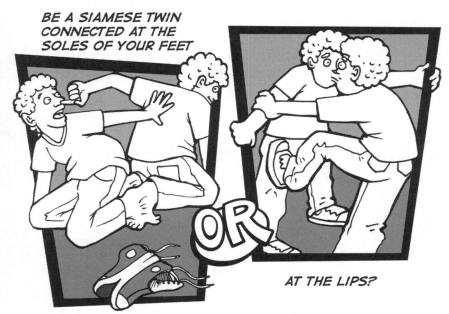

OR

AT THE LIPS?

Would you...

tackle an 80 year-old for no reason for $1,000 bucks? If you got $1,000 for every 80+ year-old you tackled in a day, how many would you go for? How would you spend the day?

Would you...

get a tattoo on every square inch of your body for two million dollars and then get it laser-removed for another two million?

Would you...

tattoo a $ sign on your scrotum for $50,000?

YOU MUST CHOOSE!

Would you rather...

your doctor spoke in Seuss rhymes...

You have six months to live:

Your heart is a pumping

Your heart is a popping

But one year in half

Your heart will be stopping

It'll clonk, it'll clank

It'll cloink, it'll clunk

And then your body will fall

Just like that — kerplunk!

And you'll be tossed in the ground

With all sorts of junk.

YOU MUST CHOOSE!

OR your boss spoke in Seuss rhymes…

You're fired.

Clean out your in-box

And jump in your out-box

Wipe clear your desk

And forget all your stox

They've been locked away

With ten thousand lox

And just for good measure

An arctic snow fox

So goodbye and sorry

If you feel disgraced

That you and three others have all been replaced

By a 16 year-old with spots on his face.

YOU MUST CHOOSE!

Would you rather...

HAVE PERMANENTLY LATHERED HAIR

OR

ONLY BE ABLE TO MOVE AROUND BY MOON-WALKING?

Would you rather...

have a speech impediment where you switch "s" and "t" sounds

OR

"p" and "w" sounds?

Things to consider: "pow-wows"; "popcorn"; "suck my tits"

Would you rather...

get facial hair on the upper half of your face

OR

have webbed thighs?

Would you rather...

recite famous historical speeches in your sleep

OR

reenact '80s sitcoms dialogue?

YOU MUST CHOOSE!

Would you rather...

when upset, always and exclusively exclaim "Consarnit"

OR

always mutter a low, long, rumbling "Sheeeeeeeyiiiiiiiiiittttttttttttt"?

Would you rather your last words be written...

by Shakespeare **OR** Dr. Seuss?

by Martin Luther King **OR** Steven Wright?

by Jesus **OR** Three 6 Mafia? Jeff Foxworthy?

Would you rather...

walk like an Egyptian

OR

walk nothing like an Egyptian, with no resemblance whatsoever in gait, stride, or posture?

YOU MUST CHOOSE!

Would you rather have your legal name be...

Balls Johnson **OR** Stubby McGraw?

Titty Watson **OR** Jackie Taint?

Fritz Nutchap Analbags **OR** Lars Scrotie-scrote Asspacket?
Things to consider: This question paraphrased from Shakespeare's *The Tempest*

Would you rather have the exact same handwriting as...

Pete Rose **OR** Joe Biden?

Kurt Cobain **OR** Leonardo da Vinci?
Things to consider: forging journals

YOU MUST CHOOSE!

Would you rather...
the upper half of your face be unable to move
OR
the left half?

Would you rather...
have a hunchback
OR
a hunchfront?

Would you rather...
have Vulcan ears
OR
a Vulcan personality?

YOU MUST CHOOSE!

Would you rather...

have an asshole for a shadow

OR

have an echo with a Canadian accent?

Would you rather...

always be bobbing and weaving like a boxer

OR

have your at-rest position be the Running Man dance?

Would you rather...

get stuck on an elevator with sweaty vaguely foreign guys

OR

DJs who want to talk incessantly about their "fat beats"?

YOU MUST CHOOSE!

Would you rather...

have whatever you are thinking Twittered to your parents every two minutes

OR

receive a Twitter with whatever your parents are thinking?

Would you rather...

be a world class sprinter but only when fully erect

OR

be a world class swimmer but only while naked?
Things to consider: pelvic thrusting at the finish line

YOU MUST CHOOSE!

If on Jeopardy, would you rather use as your question format...

"Is that a _____ in your pants or are you just happy to see me?"

OR

"You want me to say _____ , don't you?"

"Should I kick your face in, Alex, or is it _____ ?"

OR

"How 'bout a little bit of _____ ?"

YOU MUST CHOOSE!

Would you rather your child join...

a theater troupe **OR** the baseball team?

the D&D club **OR** choir?

a cooking class **OR** the Boy Scouts?

Things to consider: The Boy Scouts have made their position on homosexuality clear. A 1991 Position Statement states: "We believe that homosexual conduct is inconsistent with the requirement in the Scout Oath that a Scout be morally straight and in the Scout Law that a Scout be clean in word and deed, and that homosexuals do not provide a desirable role model for Scouts." That's right, God forbid any gay people get in the way of the manly Boy Scouts as they bedeck themselves in ascots and earn patches for craftwork to be sewn on their green felt sashes. If you're gonna act gay, accept gays. Next caller.

Would you rather have Dick Cheney's...

literal heart

OR

figurative heart?

YOU MUST CHOOSE!

Would you rather...

conduct all conversation with your partner in the tone of local newscast banter

OR

in the tone of a morning zoo show?

Things to consider: sound effects, wacky guests, "That's great Sheila. (Chuckle) Now turning our attention to the children..."

Would you rather...

be blow-dried to death

OR

slow-baked to death on a tanning bed?

Things to consider: corpse appearance for funeral

YOU MUST CHOOSE!

Would you rather...

tongue bathe every Skeeball from a Chuck E. Cheese

OR

handwash the laundry at the *Rock of Love* mansion?

Would you rather...

suffer from ingrown eyelashes

OR

eyeball warts?

Would you rather...

upon making any mistake, have someone appear who always sarcastically slow-claps to rub it in

OR

be unable to drink a beverage without doing a spit take on the first sip?

Things to consider: state dinners, wedding toasts, first dates

YOU MUST CHOOSE!

Would you rather...

emit the sound of nails on a blackboard whenever you scratch an itch

OR

cry like a three year-old when something doesn't go your way?

Would you rather...

slide under your covers, only to discover a dozen roaches scurrying about

OR

sit on the toilet, only to discover a rat swimming around?

Would you rather...

use a power drill as a Q-Tip

OR

get a lower back tattoo with lemon juice?

YOU MUST CHOOSE!

Would you rather...

get a Superglue facial

OR

use Superglue as a sexual lubricant?

Would you rather...

have a navel with a Magic 8-Ball readout in it

OR

have barbecue sauce saliva?

Things to consider: combining belly-dancing with fortune-telling, ribs

Would you rather...

bite into a popsicle with your front teeth 50 times

OR

get a paper cut on your eye?

YOU MUST CHOOSE!

Would you rather...

always look like you're severely constipated

OR

always be miming trying to keep a basketball spinning on your finger?

Would you rather...

grow an extra one inch layer of flesh for every year of your life like a tree grows wood

OR

shed your skin and hair every autumn?

Would you rather...

consume a mouse smoothie

OR

a tarantula wrap?

YOU MUST CHOOSE!

Would you rather...

have your nipples dipped in liquid nitrogen and shattered

OR

your earlobes clipped off with garden hedgers?

Would you rather...

eat Squirrel Intestine Alfredo

OR

a Bull Testicle Parmigiana sandwich?

Would you rather...

have Meg Ryan's cosmetic surgeon

OR

Tom Cruise's spiritual advisor?

YOU MUST CHOOSE!

Would you rather...

dive through a Slip-N-Slide covered in sheep excrement and urine

OR

get a Mentos and Diet Coke enema?

Would you rather...

speak like a wise Native American chief whenever you're chilly

OR

sprout facial hair at the first sign of traffic, with it getting worse as road congestion does?

Would you rather...

have the arm waddle of the world's fattest woman

OR

have the varicose leg veins of the world's oldest woman?
Things to consider: possible flight?

YOU MUST CHOOSE!

Would you rather...

invariably get stuck behind someone at least a foot taller than you at every movie, concert, play, etc.

OR

invariably get stuck behind Slowface Johnson whenever you need to get somewhere fast on the street, at an airport, etc.?

Would you rather...

have a perpetual watch glint shining in your eyes

OR

be compelled to whistle "Camptown Races" whenever seeing something purple?

Would you rather...

have literal crow's feet around your eyes

OR

have Chuck Woolery photoshopped into all of your wedding photos?

YOU MUST CHOOSE!

Which Blues song would you rather hear...

"I Didn't Get into Harvard (But I Did Get into Brown, my Safety School)"

OR

"Grass Stains Ain't Coming Out"?

Would you rather...

take your measurements 34-28-35 (for example) and have them randomly mixed up

OR

gain 5 pounds in one random place on your body?

Would you rather...

have a type of Tourette's Syndrome that causes you to exclaim "Yeah, Boyeeee!" every twenty minutes

OR

that causes you to exclaim "Here, Diagonally!"?

YOU MUST CHOOSE!

Would you rather...

have to make your Number 2s in the shower

OR

in mail slots?

Would you rather...

bitch slap a polar bear

OR

spit in the eye of a tiger?

YOU MUST CHOOSE!

Would you rather...

have cankles (no distinction between your calves and ankles)

OR

a nin (no distinction between your neck and chin)?

Would you rather permanently speak...

'70s jive

OR

CSI: Miamese (a language based on David Caruso's wry comments and bad puns)?

Things to consider: "Up top, Blood!"; "It's about time this garbage man... gets recycled."

YOU MUST CHOOSE!

FAIRLY EXTREME

AUTHORS' DEBATE

Would you rather...

your genitalia was located on the palm of your hand

Neck – Justin Heimberg

One word. Ascot. It can just be kind of your thing. With neckitals®, you can combine the ecstasy of eating with the ecstasy of sex—if you swallow just right, applying gentle pressure to the underside of the neck, you can stimulate your g-spot. If your junk was on your hands, be you a woman or man, you'd have to always explain why you are wearing that one mitten and why you aren't applauding after a show; or worse, you will applaud, hurting or arousing yourself with each clap until your mitten gets soiled. Plus, through rigorous sex, one of your arms would become way more muscular than the other, making you grotesquely asymmetrical (as if having hand genitals wasn't bad enough).

YOU MUST CHOOSE!

OR the front of your neck?

Hand it over – David Gomberg

Imagine sex. On your hand, you have all kinds of maneuverability. With neck-nuts, you're relegated to lying down and letting someone ride or thrust against you until you can't breathe. And yes, you can hide your hand genitals with a mitten and learn to write with the other hand. But neck balls, those are tough to hide (as is neck labia.) In fact being a woman is particularly distasteful in that with each intercourse thrust, you're getting a mouthful of mantuft™. And you won't develop asymmetrical muscles, because, on one hand (literally), you have the goods to have sex with; and on the other hand, literally sort of, you'd be using it to stimulate yourself during self-pleasure. Yin and yang. The balance of life.

FAIRLY EXTREME

YOU MUST CHOOSE!

EXTRA EXTREMELY EXTREME EXTRAS:
Read this page if stoned.

Flounder Flounder Flounder Flounder Flounder Flounder Flounder
Flounder Flounder Flounder Flounder Flounder Flounder Flounder
Flounder Flounder Flounder Flounder Flounder Flounder Flounder
Flounder Flounder Flounder Flounder Flounder Flounder Flounder
Flounder Flounder Flounder Flounder Flounder Flounder Flounder
Flounder Flounder Flounder Flounder Flounder Flounder Flounder
Flounder Flounder Flounder Flounder Flounder Flounder Flounder
Flounder Flounder Flounder Flounder Flounder Flounder Flounder
Flounder Flounder Flounder Flounder Flounder Flounder Flounder
Flounder Flounder Flounder Flounder Flounder Flounder Flounder
Flounder Flounder Flounder Flounder Flounder Flounder Flounder
Flounder Flounder Flounder Flounder Flounder Flounder Flounder
Flounder Flounder Flounder Flounder Flounder Flounder Flounder
Flounder Flounder Flounder Flounder Flounder Phlounder Flounder
Flounder Flounder Flounder Flounder Flounder Flounder Flounder
Flounder Flounder Flounder Flounder Flounder Flounder Flounder
Flounder Flounder Flounder Flounder Flounder Flounder Flounder
Flounder Flounder Flounder Flounder Flounder Flounder Flounder
Flounder Flounder Flounder Flounder Flounder Flounder Flounder
Flounder Flounder Flounder Flounder Flounder Flounder Flounder
Flounder Flounder Flounder Flounder Flounder Flounder Flounder

Would you rather...

ONLY BE ABLE TO EAT ORANGE FOODS

OR

ONLY BE ABLE TO EAT FOOD STARTING WITH THE LETTER "K"?

CHAPTER FIVE

EXTREMELY GROSS AND EXTREMELY EMBARRASSING

Pain is one thing, but the nausea of a gross undertaking or the emotional agony of an embarrassing situation can be even worse. To the extreme! Damn it, that didn't quite work. We've got to get the hang of this "to the extreme" thing, eventually. Jeez. Anyway, take a dive into the downright disgusting mixed with the awful and awkward... to the... never mind.

Would you rather...

eat a jelly doughnut full of snot

OR

a danish iced with yak semen?

Would you rather...

your photo was used on a herpes medication billboard

OR

for an ad for a gay dating site?

Would you rather...

have masturbated to Internet porn only to realize you left on the Skype video conference with your mom

OR

find out all of your drunk dials have been recorded and posted on iTunes?

YOU MUST CHOOSE!

Would you rather...

throw up in zero gravity

OR

have to unclog a toilet with your bare hands?

Would you rather...

consume a sundae of pig stomach dolloped with hot vomit sprinkled with mice droppings topped with the testicle of a gnu

OR

a drink a grande fecesccino?

Would you rather...

watch your grandparents' sloppy make-out/grope session

OR

discover they are watching yours lasciviously?

YOU MUST CHOOSE!

Would you rather...

brush your teeth nightly for six months with a copious inch-long portion of smegma

OR

change your name to Smegma?

Would you rather...

French kiss someone four times your age

OR

French kiss a goat?

Would you rather...

bathe in a tub of maggots

OR

fat drained from liposuction patients?

YOU MUST CHOOSE!

Would you rather...

have to wear clothes taken daily from _____ 's
dirty hamper

(insert least hygienic acquaintance)

OR

sleep each night in a bed recently "occupied" by _____ ?

(insert most sexually deviant friend)

Would you rather...

give a drunken wedding toast at your sibling's wedding where you keep
talking about how hot her friends are

OR

witness and cringe to a wedding toast from your dad that has
numerous sexual stories and graphic sexual imagery?

Would you rather...

have to milk a cow with your mouth until a bucket is full

OR

do the same by squeezing your butt cheeks?

YOU MUST CHOOSE!

Would you rather...

have a plate of human skin Carpaccio

OR

drink a glass of aged room temperature anal sweat?

Would you rather...

vomit on the floor while letting loose with diarrhea in the toilet

OR

let loose with diarrhea on the floor while vomiting in the toilet?

Things to consider: Question excerpted from Descartes' *Discourse on Method, Meditations on First Philosophy*

Would you rather...

let a cockroach crawl in your mouth and down your throat

OR

up your nose and out the other nostril?

YOU MUST CHOOSE!

Would you rather...

eat four scoops of hair from a barber shop floor and then cough up a cigar-shaped hairball like a cat

OR

eat a regurgitated cat hairball?

Would you rather...

swallow battery acid and pass it through your bladder and urethra Franklin

OR

eat several throwing stars and pass them all the way through your digestive system through your rectum?

Would you rather...

eat a soft serve cone of dog feces

OR

"Shake and Bake" litter-encrusted cat dung?

YOU MUST CHOOSE!

Would you rather...

use used Kleenex to wipe your ass

OR

use used toilet paper to blow your nose?

Would you rather...

lick clean the inside of a horse's nostril

OR

hand-clean the dingleberries of a grumpy St. Bernard? An irritable donkey? Ray Liotta?

Would you rather...

eat a pubic hair cotton candy

OR

a poopsicle?

YOU MUST CHOOSE!

Would you rather...

do a shot of bull semen

OR

taste a spoonful of horse afterbirth?

Would you rather...

wring out ten maxipads straight into your mouth

OR

receive a fire hose enema?

Would you rather...

go to a dentist with Parkinson's

OR

a proctologist with Parkinson's?

YOU MUST CHOOSE!

Would you rather...

be caught masturbating by your grandfather

OR

vice-versa? Grandmother? Nipsey Russel?

Would you rather eat ice cream flavored...

Salmon Chunk **OR** Bubble Gum (with already chewed wads)

Broccoli Sorbet **OR** Dirty Coins N' Cream?

Post Nasal Drip Swirl **OR** Roadkill Fudge?

Newsprint **OR** Ku Klux Kreme?

YOU MUST CHOOSE!

Would you rather...

kiss your grandmother goodbye, only to have her slip you the tongue

OR

bite into a turkey kielbasa, only to discover veins?

Would you rather...

have to eat like a baby bird where your mom regurgitates partially digested food into your mouth

OR

only be able to eat food that has been partially digested and excreted by some living thing?

Would you rather...

find a condom at the bottom of your vanilla milkshake

OR

sip a bowl of gazpacho only to discover a pubic hair at the bottom?

YOU MUST CHOOSE!

125

Would you rather...

eat a sushi roll of a maggot-encrusted slug

OR

eat a caramel apple rolled on the floor of a barber shop?

Would you rather have a bird crap...

in your hair **OR** on your new car?

in your ear **OR** all over your clothes?

in your eye **OR** in your mouth?

YOU MUST CHOOSE!

EXTRA EXTREMELY EXTREME EXTRAS:
Increasingly Egregious Misspellings Of Hanukah

Hannukah

Chanukaha

Ghananka

Chunkyka

Honkeykah

Donkeykong

YOU MUST CHOOSE!

C H A P T E R SIX

UNEXTREME POWERS

Okay, so the truth is that these powers are not necessarily extreme. They tend to fall a little short of "super" as superpowers go. Nonetheless, will you use these extremely unextreme abilities for good or evil? You, and you alone, must choose… *to the unextreme!*

Would you rather...

be spared the annoyance of magazines' inserted subscription cards

OR

have pinpoint TiVo stopping accuracy?

Would you rather...

poop fragrant potpourri bundles

OR

have permanent Listerine breath?

Things to consider: romance, defecating in crystal bowls

Would you rather...

have an hour-long chat with your 12 year-old self

OR

with your 72 year-old self?

YOU MUST CHOOSE!

Would you rather...

be able to scan documents into your computer with your tongue

OR

be able to weed-whack with your foot?

Would you rather...

have Thomas Dewey (of Decimal System fame) as your personal organizer

OR

George Washington Carver as your personal chef?

Would you rather...

have lemon-flavored hangnails

OR

naturally scab corduroy?

YOU MUST CHOOSE!

Which iPod app would you want...

one that takes a picture of someone and then spits back which celebrity they look most like **OR** a Zagat-like public restroom guide?

one that makes the phone edible **OR** one that emits a blinding ray?

one that makes disco ball lights **OR** iRazor, where you can shave your face with the screen?

iGina **OR** iSoapdispenser?

iLiner **OR** iBrator?

Would you rather...

your dreams were written by Roald Dahl
OR
Judd Apatow?

YOU MUST CHOOSE!

Would you rather...

have the UPS commercial guy's doodling ability but also have his hair

OR

have the old Fed-Ex guy's speed-talking ability but also have his mustache?

Would you rather...

have self-lathering skin

OR

refrigerated pockets?

Would you rather...

have a yarmulke with razor sharp edges that you use to fight off bad guys like the guy in James Bond's *Goldfinger*

OR

be able to fight and kill with office supplies?

YOU MUST CHOOSE!

Would you rather...

be able to automatically dictate your actual mood just by selecting a MySpace emoticon

OR

instantly be doing whatever you change your Facebook status to?

Would you rather...

be able to come in fourth in any race any time

OR

be able to high jump at an Olympic level but only when dressed in the shorts-on-the-outside-of-the-sweatpants look?

YOU MUST CHOOSE!

Would you rather...

have multiple lives like a video game character in Donkey Kong

OR

have multiple weapons as in Halo?

Would you rather...

be effortlessly flawless at Whack-a-Mole

OR

be able to perfectly forge anyone's handwriting but only when writing the phrase "I want pudding!"

Things to consider: selling forged Obama signed photos

Would you rather...

be a supervillain called the Grammarian (weapons shaped like punctuation marks, perfectly expressed diabolical speeches, constantly correcting the grammar of your foes)

OR

The Doorman? (weapons include keys and door knobs; always engaging in trivial polite conversation as you kill foes).

YOU MUST CHOOSE!

Would you rather...

have unlimited texting

OR

permission for unlimited farting?

Would you rather...

have a pet Pegasus, but one with a personality that is very "dickish"

OR

have a centaur friend who is constantly shamelessly hitting on you?

Would you rather...

be immune to "order envy"

OR

have "The Yellow Rose of Texas" emanate whenever you urinate?

YOU MUST CHOOSE!

Would you rather...

be able to "Billie Jean" sidewalk squares and floor tiles

OR

have your fingernails cultivated and shaped into lock picks?

Would you rather...

have your peeled dead skin taste like cherry fruit roll-up

OR

be able to defecate complex domino set ups?

YOU MUST CHOOSE!

INVENTOIDS BY MERLE PELSBORP

Would you rather...

have a bed that heats on one side but not the other
(to mitigate male-female disparity)

OR

have a "toilet blender" (a garbage disposal for your toilet
to prevent clogs)?

Would you rather...

have the ability to swap facial features with friends

OR

have the freedom to swap sexual partners with no emotional
or moral fall-out?

YOU MUST CHOOSE!

Would you rather be reincarnated as...

a rabbit **OR** a snake?

a Midwestern farmer **OR** an Ivy League a capella singer?

an average accountant **OR** the character of Charles in
"Charles in Charge"?

Would you rather...

have heightened intuition in Rock Paper Scissors

OR

be able to increase the speeds of escalators?

Would you rather...

have a daily allowance of 10,000 calories with no weight gain

OR

have the ability to induce instant and intense diarrhea in anyone
you wish?

Things to consider: public debates, dinner parties

YOU MUST CHOOSE!

Would you rather...

be able to personally choose every member of the Supreme Court

OR

every Oscar winner?

Things to consider: Chief Justice Björk

Would you rather...

always appear half your age

OR

3/4 of your weight?

Would you rather...

have a belly button vortex that sucks objects within two inches into nothingness

OR

be a supervillain called the Mime, who can mime objects into existence?

Would you rather...

never miss a shot when playing quarters

OR

have unlimited quarters?

YOU MUST CHOOSE!

Would you rather...

have the freckles on your back form a perfect astrological map

OR

have your pulse beat to the guitar riff of "Sunshine of Your Love"?

Would you rather...

be able to pop popcorn kernels in your closed fist

OR

have your Bluetooth headset snap into your navel?

Would you rather...

tan in the pattern of desert camouflage

OR

have nostrils that dispense mustard and ketchup
when you blow your nose?

Things to consider: military career, what if it were dessert camouflage

YOU MUST CHOOSE!

Would you rather...

be able to Twitter updates straight into subscribers' brains

OR

be able to receive Twitter updates the same way?

Would you rather...

be able to spit tobacco with pinpoint accuracy up to fifty feet

OR

be able to fart to the tune of the opening to any song?

Would you rather...

be able to understand quantum physics

OR

be able to prove via geometrical proof that Baby does indeed got back?

YOU MUST CHOOSE!

Would you rather...

have a pocket in the skin of your thigh

OR

have a working zip-up change purse for a scrotum?

Things to consider: the beach

Would you rather...

have a photographic memory where you remember everything you see

OR

have a phonographic memory where you remember everything you hear with a scratchy slightly high pitched old-timey sound?

Would you rather...

be able to dry yourself without a towel by shaking like a dog

OR

be able to lick your nuts like said dog?

YOU MUST CHOOSE!

Would you rather...

be able to perform electrolysis with your finger tips

OR

be able to type your thoughts by resting your head
on your computer keyboard?

Would you rather...

have a thumb that dispenses moisturizer

OR

have nipples that can act as cigarette lighters?

Would you rather...

have eyes that can change color to best match your outfit

OR

be able to change your race on command?

YOU MUST CHOOSE!

Would you rather...

be able to shake off unwanted hair like a wet dog

OR

be able to reposition fat cells like squeezing a tube of toothpaste?

Would you rather...

(Men read as have a partner with...)
have a naturally Brazilian butt

OR

a naturally Brazilian wax job?

Would you rather have...

relationship precognition (know everything that's about to happen)

OR

relationship postcognition (know everything your partner has done)?

YOU MUST CHOOSE!

AUTHORS' DEBATE

Would you rather...

HAVE PARMESAN CHEESE DANDRUFF

OR

BUBBLE WRAP ACNE?

That's a wrap—Justin Heimberg

There are few joys as orgasmically enjoyable as popping bubble wrap. It's irresistibly satisfying. There is something primal about it. It goes back to our evolutionary need to pinch grain or something. Every human has the instinct. Anytime you're bored, you can just pop a bubble zit and get that crackle of satisfaction, either one at a time, or if you have a rather bad breakout, a bunch at once. So, your face will look like a cross between Edward James Olmos and phone packaging. Big deal. Your bubble-pocked face will be smiling ear to ear in joy.

Cheese Please—David Gomberg

Bubble wrap acne has no function. It is a useless deformity. Parmesan cheese dandruff, on the other hand, is wonderfully utilitarian. Parmesan goes well on anything, and a little goes a long way. So if you're out in a restaurant and you get some chicken parmesan, all it takes is a shake of the head, and you're good. Who wants to be addicted to popping their own face? People go through years of therapy for that. Pizza, pasta, vegetables all come alive with a little of the magic from your head and shoulders.

CHAPTER SEVEN

CELEBRITIES AND POP CULTURE (TO THE EXTREME, INCIDENTALLY)

Our extreme culture has an extreme obsession with extreme celebrity.
Extremely so. How many communal hours of potential productivity
have been sacrificed to worship those who are famous merely for doing
something extreme, be it garish displays of wealth or masochistic acts
on skateboards? It's time to put that pop culture addiction to use and
choose between two famous-folk fates.

Would you rather...

talk like Donald Trump

OR

have his hair?

Would you rather...

always speak to the rhythm of "My Girl Likes to Party All the Time"

OR

to the tune of "Hey Mickey"?

Would you rather...

have the *Saturday Night Live* guy appear to introduce you whenever you meet new people

OR

have the voice in your head sound like Optimus Prime?

YOU MUST CHOOSE!

Would you rather...

look like Gene Simmons

OR

think like him?

Would you rather...

be a Siamese twin with Nicole Richie

OR

LeBron James?

Would you rather...

have your mom and her friends star on a reality show called "Real Housewives of (Your Home City)"

OR

not?

YOU MUST CHOOSE!

Would you rather...

make out with Tila Tequila

OR

slap her?

Would you rather your mom be...

Marge Simpson **OR** Lois Griffin?

Peg Bundy **OR** Carol Brady?

Morticia Addams **OR** Ann Coulter?

Would you rather your dad be...

Bill Clinton **OR** Richard Gere?

Ru Paul **OR** Ron Paul?

Hulk Hogan **OR** Gandalf?

YOU MUST CHOOSE!

Would you rather spend a long car ride with...

the Real Housewives of New Jersey **OR** the Real Housewives of Orange County?

Jared of Subway fame **OR** the Hamburglar?

Plato **OR** Tiger Woods?

Would you rather...

have Jessica Simpson's intellect

OR

Jessica Alba's insatiable need (and respective inability) to be funny?
Things to consider: how difficult Alba makes it for men to masturbate to her in her comedies

YOU MUST CHOOSE!

Would you rather be trapped as a character inside...

Gossip Girl **OR** *Grey's Anatomy?*

Lost **OR** *The View?*

The A-Team **OR** *The Office?*

Would you rather...

have to sit through a drunken tirade from Mel Gibson

OR

a serious religious sermon from Tom Cruise?

Would you rather elect as president...

Sarah Palin

OR

Tina Fey?

YOU MUST CHOOSE!

Would you rather...

only be able to leave voicemails in the style and manner of an angry Alec Baldwin

OR

only be able to get your hair cut in the style of an angst-ridden Britney Spears?

Would you rather...

know the truth behind every aspect of Michael Jackson's life

OR

not?

Would you rather...

sit on a transatlantic flight next to Will Ferrell

OR

Oprah?

Things to consider: conversation, mutual armrest competition

YOU MUST CHOOSE!

Would you rather...

have a star on the Walk of Fame

OR

have a deli sandwich named after you?

Would you rather...

have James Taylor living in your closet to help sing your children to sleep

OR

have Pantera in the closet to help wake them up?

Would you rather attempt to solve...

the atrocities in Darfur with Jennifer Love Hewitt

OR

Planck's Constant with Matt LeBlanc?

Would you rather...

play Mastermind with Morgan Freeman

OR

make an omelet with Gloria Estefan?

YOU MUST CHOOSE!

Would you rather...

have to marry someone at least 40 years your elder like Soon-Yi did with Woody Allen

OR

20 years your younger like Demi Moore did with Ashton Kutcher?

Things to consider: immaturity, gray pubes

Would you rather...

always have the intense facial expression of a runway model

OR

always have the eerie smiling expression of the Burger King mascot?

Would you rather...

have to get everywhere by Green Machine

OR

by a ball hopper?

YOU MUST CHOOSE!

Would you rather...

have Wolverine hair

OR

wolverine hair?

Would you rather...

be the personal assistant to Donald Trump

OR

Naomi Campbell?

Things to consider: getting fired, getting tired

Would you rather...

be stuck in a bomb shelter with 100 math nerds

OR

with Emeril Lagasse and Joan Rivers?

YOU MUST CHOOSE!

Would you rather have been a fly on the wall...

while Hugh Grant was soliciting Divine Brown **OR** while Eddie Murphy was soliciting that transsexual prostitute?

in the Oval Office with President Clinton and Monica Lewinsky **OR** the first meetings of Brad Pitt and Angelina Jolie?

while Michael Jackson had any of his various sleepovers with any of his various sleepover guests **OR** during OJ's infamous visit to Nicole Brown's townhouse?

Would you rather...

be raised by *Jon and Kate plus 8*

OR

the Kardashians?

YOU MUST CHOOSE!

Would you rather...

move like a dancing Gwen Stefani whenever you walk

OR

sway and stomp like Dave Matthews when standing?

Would you rather...

have Popeye's forearms

OR

his cheeks? How about his mental retardation/speech problems or his horrid violent temper and probable alcoholism?

Would you rather...

have permanent Dizzy Gillespie cheeks

OR

speak in jazz scat?

YOU MUST CHOOSE!

Would you rather upon meeting new people...

always cheek-kiss **OR** high five?

hug **OR** low ten?

do that thing where you lock hands and look in and it looks like a vagina **OR** flex your biceps and sing baritone doo-wop á la ShaNaNa's Bowser?

Would you rather...

be forced to have product placement in your conversations
OR
have to spell out all the words you speak?

Would you rather...

be able to travel via personal Segway
OR
with blades that emerge from your hat,
Inspector Gadget style?

YOU MUST CHOOSE!

Would you rather...

be bcc'ed on every email to and from Hillary Clinton **OR** Kobe Bryant?

Jennifer Aniston **OR** Ozzy Osbourne?

the Olsen twins **OR** Weird Al Yankovic?

Would you rather...

have to conduct all business meetings in a Spencer's Gifts
OR
in a car parked at Inspiration Point?

Would you rather fight to the death...

a group of sports mascots **OR** cereal mascots?

the last panda on earth **OR** your least favorite relative?

500 possessed protractors **OR** 50 Monchichis?

YOU MUST CHOOSE!

Would you rather...

name your kids something weird and pretentious like celebrities often do

OR

name them "La'Your Name'"?

Things to consider: Which celebrity baby name do you like/hate most?

Would you rather...

have everything you eat taste like Bit-O-Honey

OR

everything you drink taste like Purplesaurus Rex Kool-Aid?

Would you rather...

have gratuitous Nick Cannon cameos in your life

OR

have the sound of studio applause emanate whenever you accomplish something or make a good decision?

YOU MUST CHOOSE!

Would you rather...

be roommates with Jack Tripper

OR

neighbors with Ray Romano?

Would you...

sell space on your body for a tattoo advertisement for $500,000?
Your gravestone? Your child's name?

Things to consider: Nike Heimberg, Abercrombie Fitch Gomberg

Would you rather...

have sex with a soft and tender Toucan Sam

OR

a freaky, furious Cocoa Puffs bird?

YOU MUST CHOOSE!

Would you rather fight to the death...

Fat Albert **OR** Simon and Garfunkel?

a possessed George Foreman grill **OR** an evil version of yourself?

one sober Jean-Claude Van Damme **OR** three drunk Jean-Claude Van Dammes?

Would you rather...

have a massive back tattoo of Mr. Belvedere

OR

a tattoo of an ampersand on your forehead?

YOU MUST CHOOSE!

Would you rather...

use a razor blade with just one blade

OR

one with 19 blades?

Would you rather...

get caught in a hailstorm of D&D dice

OR

poppers?

YOU MUST CHOOSE!

Would you rather always have to wear...

an eye patch **OR** a nicotine patch?

a snowboard **OR** a Wonder Twins outfit?

Ferrari glasses **OR** Ferraro glasses (Geraldine)?

Would you rather your graduation speaker be...

Paris Hilton **OR** Gallagher?

Dennis Miller **OR** a happy Asian guy who barely speaks English?

Barack Obama **OR** Optimus Prime?
Things to consider: "Class of 2012, Roll out!"

YOU MUST CHOOSE!

167

AUTHORS' DEBATE

Would you rather...

HAVE SEX WITH CELEBRITIES
WITH LAST NAMES THAT
BEGIN WITH "L"

OR

LAST NAMES THAT
BEGIN WITH "B"?

L—Justin Heimberg

Lohan, Liu, Lawless, Landry, Lavigne, Lindvall, Lima, Longoria, Lopez, Borgnine

B2B—David Gomberg

Biel, Bellucci, Bundchen, Braxton, Bullock, Barrymore, Banks, Beckham, Big-ones, Lundgren

EXTRA EXTREMELY EXTREME EXTRAS:

Things to Give Kids on Halloween to Disappoint Them

Miniature alcohol bottles like they have on airplanes

Lamb chops

Autographed photographs of Federal Reserve Chairman Ben Bernanke

A ladleful of gravy

A deed to a fictional ranch

Silks and spices the likes of which they've never seen

Shaving scum

Flotsam and/or Jetsam

Spalding Gray Monologue tapes

YOU MUST CHOOSE!

CHAPTER EIGHT

EXTREMELY FEMININE

The following questions are extreme enough for a man, but PH-balanced for a woman. If you're a dude, turn to the next chapter. *To the extreme!* Or if in mixed company, pay attention to the answers so you can understand what women really want.

Would you rather...

never fight with your partner

OR

fight once a week and have great make-up sex?

Would you rather...

have a compulsion that causes you to invariably refer to your breasts as "my jiggle set"

OR

always refer to your vagina as "my love canyon"?

Things to consider: doctor's appointments, writing love letters, getting work at Penthouse

Would you rather have a partner with...

a perfect face **OR** a 9-inch penis?

a 2-inch wide, 3-inch long penis **OR** a half-inch wide, 10-inch long penis?

a ribbed-for-your-pleasure penis **OR** a snake tongue?

YOU MUST CHOOSE!

Would you rather...

have sex with John Goodman

OR

assume his weight?

Would you rather...

have sex with Ben Affleck if he gained 50 pounds

OR

Ashton Kutcher if he was speaking the entire time?

Would you rather...

buy seven cucumbers and three boxes of Vagisil at the supermarket right in front of your neighbor

OR

be a nude model for a kindergarten art class?

YOU MUST CHOOSE!

Would you rather...

own a pair of heels that adjusted to flats with the push of a button

OR

a handbag that was able to carry up to 100 pounds without feeling any heavier?

Would you rather...

be smacked in the face with an Andy Roddick serve and then make out with him

OR

get kicked in the stomach by David Beckham and then grope each other feverishly?

Would you rather fart...

in front of your husband/boyfriend **OR** in front of your parents?

in front of your infant child **OR** your pet?

in front of Dame Judi Dench **OR** the ghost of Thomas Jefferson?

YOU MUST CHOOSE!

Would you rather...

have "man hands"

OR

"man feet"?

Would you rather have breasts the consistency of...

softballs **OR** partially-wadded tin foil?

a bag of Frosted Flakes **OR** a sack of wine?

soap bubbles **OR** solid brass?

Would you rather...

have an upside-down vagina **OR** a horizontal vagina?

two vaginas **OR** an anus and vagina that have switched places?

a vagina that can act as a blowdryer **OR** a vacuum?

YOU MUST CHOOSE!

Would you rather...

get in a catfight with Miley Cyrus

OR

Ne-Ne from *Real Housewives: Atlanta*?

Would you rather...

find out your coveted collection of Jimmy Choo handbags were all cheap knock-offs

OR

your real designer bags were made by slave-like child labor?

Would you rather...

be caricatured by Kristen Wiig on *Saturday Night Live*

OR

have *Us Weekly* regularly photograph you and make fun of your wardrobe in its *Fashion Police* section?

YOU MUST CHOOSE!

Would you rather...

have your boobs drop six inches overnight

OR

your butt drop six inches overnight?

Would you rather...

get a haircut in the style of Dorothy Hamill

OR

Dorothy from *The Wizard of Oz*?

Would you rather...

on your wedding day, accidentally say an old boyfriend's name during your vows

OR

after walking down the aisle to make your entrance, realize you have skidmarks on your wedding dress?

YOU MUST CHOOSE!

Would you rather...

fellate a guy with a 14-inch penis while you're suffering from a sore throat

OR

receive anal sex from a guy with a 2-inch diameter penis?

Things to consider: This question excerpted from Chaucer's *Canterbury Tales*

Would you rather...

have sex with Mel Gibson **OR** Kevin Federline?

John Mayer **OR** Ryan Reynolds?

Josh Groban **OR** Kanye West?

the character of Dr. House **OR** the character of Chuck from *Gossip Girl*?

a sea lion **OR** Dick Cheney?

YOU MUST CHOOSE!

Would you rather...

have the ability to instantly make your breasts the size of your choice

OR

have a butt capable of altering size and shape to fit into any pair of pants (but only while you are wearing the pants)?

Things to consider: disrobing for sex, jogging

Would you rather...

your partner have a one-inch penis

OR

the most perfect penis; however it's jutting out of his lower back? His neck? The bottom of his left foot?

Would you rather...

tattoo Bret Michaels's name on your forehead

OR

have unprotected sex with him and just hope for the best?

YOU MUST CHOOSE!

Would you rather...

at bars, constantly be hit on by every guy no matter how lame he is

OR

always have to make the first move?

DATE, MARRY, OR SCREW?

Tom Cruise, Johnny Depp, Barack Obama

Anderson Cooper, the Pick-Up Artist, Seth Rogen

Michael Kors, Tom Colicchio, The Incredible Hulk

YOU MUST CHOOSE!

Would you...

never send another text message to have sex with George Clooney?

Would you...

eat your next 50 meals at McDonald's to grope Justin Timberlake?

Would you...

have your breasts surgically altered so that one was a B-cup and the other was a DDD-cup to have Josh Hartnett as a sex slave?

YOU MUST CHOOSE!

Would you rather suffer the fate of...

Joan of Arc

OR

Katie Holmes?

Would you rather...

have self-renewing shoes

OR

have self-applying make-up?

Would you rather your boyfriend be...

Cojo **OR** Steve-O?

Dwight Yoakam **OR** Dwight Schrute?

Michael Phelps **OR** Criss Angel?

Would you rather...

have Amy Winehouse's drug problems

OR

her fashion problems?

YOU MUST CHOOSE!

182

Would you rather...

be the fourth Kardashian sister

OR

the third Hilton sister?

Would you rather...

hook up with everyone Nicole Kidman has ever hooked up with

OR

everyone Jennifer Aniston has ever hooked up with?

Would you rather...

have Kim Kardashian's ass but uncontrollably fart all the time

OR

Salma Hayek's breasts but uncontrollably lactate all the time?

Would you rather...

receive a new piece of Tiffany's jewelry every month

OR

receive oral sex from Colin Farrell on your command?

YOU MUST CHOOSE!

Would you rather live in a world...

where women earned on average 25% more than men

OR

where men experienced menstrual cycles, symptoms and cramps?

Would you rather live in a world...

where men took their wives' last names upon marriage

OR

where couples chose a new last name together?

Things to consider: Maury Chung, Matthew Parker, Mr. and Mrs. Lightning

Would you rather have a 3-way with...

Ben and Casey Affleck **OR** Mark and Donnie Wahlberg?

Fred and Ben Savage **OR** Jerry and Charlie O'Connell?

Noel and Liam Gallagher **OR** the AFLAC Duck and
the Kool-Aid Man?

YOU MUST CHOOSE!

Would you rather permanently ban the word...

"ho" **OR** "dyke"?

"panties" **OR** "bromance"?

the C-word **OR** the N-word?

"windy" **OR** "challenge"?

If it meant having a flawless body, would you give up...

eating utensils?

vowels?

carbon-based sexual partners?

YOU MUST CHOOSE!

Would you rather...

if forced to do so on national TV, with your current abilities, have the chance to nationally disprove the "women are bad drivers" stereotype

OR

the "bad at math" stereotype?

Would you rather...

be able to manicure nails by sucking on fingers

OR

pedicure nails by sucking on toes?
Things to consider: doing your own nails, working at a salon

Would you rather...

have access to the world's only honest mechanic

OR

the world's hottest gynecologist?

YOU MUST CHOOSE!

Would you rather...

have an index finger that blended perfect margaritas and other mixed drinks

OR

have card-shuffling cleavage?

Would you rather...

have your significant other love to sleep, holding, cuddling, and touching you

OR

never have blanket tugging issues?

Would you rather...

receive an all-expense paid trip to Paris but have your travel partner be a two year-old child you have to look after

OR

spend a luxury private-island escape in Fiji with the two Coreys?

YOU MUST CHOOSE!

Would you rather...

be able to cause couples to break up by focusing your negative energy on them

OR

be capable of causing couples to form?

Would you rather...

have towelettes that can wipe away wrinkles

OR

ones that can wipe away memories of bad relationships?

Would you rather...

the National Debt Clock in Times Square instead display your weight at all times

OR

the JumboTron at Madison Square Garden play a video of your daily grooming and waxing?

YOU MUST CHOOSE!

Would you rather...

only be able to have sex with John Goodman until you orgasm in the act

OR

only be allowed to eat dice until you pooped a 7?

Would you rather...

be the CEO of a Fortune 500 company

OR

the wife of one?

Things to consider: Be honest

Would you rather...

work off of a computer from 1978

OR

have to dress in the fashion of 1978?

Things to consider: green text, green bellbottoms

YOU MUST CHOOSE!

Would you rather...

work under 1985 office dress codes

OR

1955 office politics?

Things to consider: feathered hair, expectant ass-slapping, "Thanks, babe!"

Without anyone finding out, would you sleep with your boss for...

a promotion?

a fully paid, 4-day work week?

a fully paid, 3-day work week?

a gorgeous private work bathroom?

a job title of "Royal Highness"?

Would you rather...

increase your annual salary by $1,000

OR

permanently reduce someone else's (your choice) by $10,000?

YOU MUST CHOOSE!

Would you rather...

have an office kitty

OR

an office hottie?

Things to consider: tongue baths, visible scratches

Would you rather...

realize after your first day at work that you were showing serious thong "whale tale"

OR

give a thoughtful presentation only to then realize you had a serious case of nipple-itis during the whole thing?

Things to consider: Both happened to Madeline Albright

Would you rather...

find out all your emails were being monitored and read by your boss

OR

that all your moments at your desk were being filmed by a security camera?

YOU MUST CHOOSE!

Would you rather...

have sex with this guy

OR this guy?

YOU MUST CHOOSE!

EXTRA EXTREMELY EXTREME EXTRAS:

5 Events if There Were an Autumn Olympics

Speed-raking

Synchronized Pumpkin Carving

Leaf Pile Floor Exercise

Cider-Mulling for Accuracy

Biathlon: Distance Run through Forest; Foliage Appreciation

YOU MUST CHOOSE!

CHAPTER NINE

EXTREMELY MASCULINE

Okay, so here's where all the extra extreme extraneous questions about balls and porn and sports fall into. What may seem a bit extreme to the fairer sex is just everyday conversation for guys. If you're a lady, you may want to move on, or you may find what guys have to say in this chapter extremely interesting... and perhaps interestingly extreme? No? Anyone? That was a nice turn of phrase. Screw you... to the extreme!

Would you rather...

get five hours of conversation with Barack Obama

OR

five minutes of wild sex with Jessica Alba?

Would you rather...

your only porn be toilet paper commercials

OR

1983 high school yearbooks?

Would you rather...

date someone on a perpetual period

OR

with perpetual PMS?

YOU MUST CHOOSE!

Would you rather...

have Internet chat sex only to find out it was your aunt (she discovers it was you too)

OR

receive a great glory hole BJ only to then realize it was former NBA great Ralph Sampson on the other side of the wall?

Would you rather...

have the old Boston Garden parquet floor in your living room

OR

a backyard that is a replica of Hole 7 at Augusta National Golf Club?

Would you rather...

have testicles that literally drag on the floor when you're naked

OR

testicles that zig and zag around wildly like nuclear particles?

Things to consider: stuffing your sock, freeballing

YOU MUST CHOOSE!

Would you rather have sex with...

Eva Mendes **OR** Alicia Keys?

Mary Louise Parker **OR** Kendra Wilkinson, but you have to talk with her for two hours before?

Heidi Klum **OR** Heidi Montag ?

Maria Sharapova with full grunting **OR** Lauren Conrad on mute?

Eva Longoria **OR** Vanessa Hudgens?

Minka Kelly **OR** Minka (the porn star/world's largest breasted Asian)?

YOU MUST CHOOSE!

Would you rather...

have a penis that could be detached and attached (with sensitivity)
to any part of your body

OR

have a penis that could be played like a flute?

Would you rather...

see you parents' room's stains exposed with a blacklight

OR

have your parents expose your room?

Things to consider: You and your parents would both be present during the reveal.

Would you rather...

when passing by people, be compelled to guard them
as if playing basketball

OR

have an insatiable compulsion to knock things out
of children's hands?

YOU MUST CHOOSE!

Would you rather...

have sex with a mermaid

OR

with a reverse mermaid (upper half = big fish, lower half = woman)?

Would you rather...

have softball-sized testicles

OR

softball-sized breasts?

Would you rather...

turn into Paul Revere during foreplay

OR

turn into Jerry Lewis upon orgasm?

Would you rather...

have self-lubricating genitals

OR

be able to dunk two-handed?

YOU MUST CHOOSE!

Would you rather...

have a bowling alley in your house

OR

have a device resembling a bowling alley ball-returner that refills empty beer mugs?

Would you rather...

see an action movie set in a Bed, Bath and Beyond

OR

at a Panera's Breads and Bakery?

Would you rather...

have penises for fingers

OR

a finger for your penis?

YOU MUST CHOOSE!

Would you rather...

have to drive three times the speed limit

OR

1/3 the speed limit?

Would you rather...

die by drowning yourself in your toilet

OR

by consuming roll after roll of Charmin?

Would you rather have sex with...

Carrie Underwood **OR** Kristen Bell?

Beyoncé **OR** Rihanna?

Danica Patrick **OR** Fergie?

your hottest high school teacher **OR** Eliza Dushku?

YOU MUST CHOOSE!

Would you rather...

have a girlfriend with speedbag breasts you could practice your boxing on

OR

with a heavy bag back?

Would you rather...

be cross-eyed

OR

cross-balled?

Would you rather...

regularly experience nocturnal emission

OR

a nocturnal admission (where once a night you admit something embarrassing in your sleep)?

YOU MUST CHOOSE!

Would you rather...

have sex with Jenna Jameson

OR

Jenna Haze

OR

Jenna Fischer?

Would you rather...

be the sixth man off the bench for an NBA team but get no money

OR

receive an NBA salary but have to keep your current job?

Would you rather fight...

a rhino with a machine gun

OR

a rabid dog without any weapons?

YOU MUST CHOOSE!

Would you rather...

have to wear a yarmulke on your head

OR

a mini yarmulke on your penis head?

Would you rather...

fight to the death Radiohead **OR** the cast of *Billy Elliot?*

Charles Barkley **OR** a barber shop quartet?

a polar bear **OR** 3 Raleigh Fingers clones?

11 possessed trombones **OR** 10,000 fire flies?

3,500 Venn diagrams **OR** the sound of a crow cawing?

Would you rather...

have a music playlist sent to you that is scientifically proven to increase exercise performance

OR

a playlist that is scientifically proven to help you get laid?

YOU MUST CHOOSE!

Would you rather...

only be able to pee on cop cars

OR

only be able to crap by flagpoles?

Would you rather date a girl with...

junk in the trunk **OR** fats in the lats?

a rose in the nose **OR** wheat in the feet?

(Pirates) maps on the traps **OR** pegs for the legs?

Would you rather...

talk like Ben Stein during sex

OR

have your partner talk like Linda Blair from *The Exorcist*?

Would you rather...

trade lives with Conan O'Brien

OR

Tiger Woods?

YOU MUST CHOOSE!

Would you rather...

have Jay Leno's money but also his chin

OR

have Letterman's money but also his outlook on life?

Would you rather...

have a panther that obeys your every command and does your bidding **OR** 500 bees that do the same?

a pack of dolphins **OR** a trio of former NBA seven footers?

a king cobra **OR** Skippy from *Family Ties*?

Would you rather...

have sex with Dakota Fanning in seven years

OR

Jennifer Love Hewitt twelve years ago?

YOU MUST CHOOSE!

PICK YOUR PENIS!
Would you rather have...

a candy cane shaped penis **OR** a corkscrew shaped penis?

a hammerhead penis **OR** a Phillips screwdriver head to your penis?

a Pez-dispensing penis **OR** a penis that shoots out a little flag that says "bang" upon orgasm?

Would you rather live in a world where...

whoever denied it, supplied it

OR

whoever smelt it, dealt it?

YOU MUST CHOOSE!

Would you rather...

fight Zach Braff

OR

Zac Efron?

Would you rather be stuck on a deserted island with...

Aristotle **OR** Megan Fox?

Dave Chappelle **OR** Sacha Baron Cohen?

Simon Cowell **OR** an electronic Simon game?
Things to consider: going mad

Tom Collichio **OR** Lindsay Lohan?

Moses **OR** Moses Malone?
Things to consider: playing one on one

YOU MUST CHOOSE!

Would you rather change your name to...

Porp **OR** Aragorn?

Narkath the Bloated **OR** Zorzootz 9?

the smell of toffee **OR** the sound of change jingling?

Would you rather...

have your cell phone set on racist joke

OR

stench of taint?

Would you rather...

have a 14 second metabolism from eating to excretion

OR

every five minutes, have the place where you're standing explode, so you got to get the hell out of there like an action hero?

Things to consider: toilet chairs, nomadic life

YOU MUST CHOOSE!

Would you rather...

only be sexually excited by thoughts of Kurt Rambis

OR

have genitalia set to explode the day you turn 70?

Would you rather...

be a man with 38DDs

OR

be a man with a one-inch penis?

Would you rather...

fight the Smurf village

OR

the full collection of Care Bears?

Things to consider: smurfberry catapults, tummy powers

YOU MUST CHOOSE!

Would you rather...

summarily execute all DJs

OR

all reality stars?

Would you rather...

have your self-esteem hinge on the L.A. Clippers road record

OR

have your happiness dependent on the bounty of an Alaskan crabbing ship?

Would you rather...

be able to park in handicap places

OR

be able to make fun of the retarded with no guilt or repercussions?

YOU MUST CHOOSE!

Would you rather...

have a Real Doll of Megan Fox

OR

a voodoo doll of your most hated male celebrity?

Would you rather...

have your profanity magically dubbed with less offensive words

OR

have everything you hear delayed like you are off reporting via satellite (you have to hold your ear to hear and nod like they do as well)?

Which of the following email addresses would you rather use...

scrotationdevice@gmail.com **OR** johnnydoodoo@aol.com?

ballslikeavocados@tmail.com **OR** saggysac@gmail.com?

fartonyourface@yahoo.com **OR** racismisok@hotmail.com?

YOU MUST CHOOSE!

Would you rather...

always deliver the perfect toast, balanced with poignancy

OR

be able to shoot pencils with your belly fat with the force and accuracy of a bow and arrow?

Would you rather...

always have a parking spot open up when you need it

OR

always be able to reach into your pocket and have exact change?

Would you rather...

be wasted at your child's birthday party

OR

your parents' anniversary dinner?

Would you...

spend ten minutes in the octagon with *Ultimate Fighting* giant Brock Lesnar for ten minutes in bed with Adriana Lima?

YOU MUST CHOOSE!

INTERNATIONAL HOUSE OF DILEMMAS

Would you rather...

eat only British food **OR** have British teeth?

have to always sit Indian style **OR** always have French B.O.?

live in a society that dressed in togas **OR** in feathered headdresses?

Would you rather...

be incredibly charming but always have a dump in your pants
OR
be extremely witty but feel compelled to intermittently spread peanut butter all over your arm?

Would you rather...

marry the Octomom
OR
be raised by her?

YOU MUST CHOOSE!

Would you rather...

write all work-related emails in the voice of an eighth grade girl full of IM abbreviations, smileys, and "like"s

OR

in the voice of a weirdly articulate revolutionary soldier's letter as in "Today at the meeting, I met a man to whose countenance men were beholden." ?

Would you rather...

have a comb-over from your chest hair

OR

ear hair? Eyelashes?

Would you rather...

have to masturbate with a mitten

OR

with your off-hand?

YOU MUST CHOOSE!

Would you rather...

when older, smoke a pipe

OR

cigars?

Gun to your head, if you had to have sex with a guy, who would you choose?

YOU MUST CHOOSE!

CHAPTER TEN

EXTREME FANTASIES

"Extreme fantasy" is a redundancy. You don't tend to have fantasies of pleasant, though unexceptional sex, and you don't dream about being the second string quarterback signaling in plays from the sidelines. Then again, to each his own. The following fantasies run the gamut from mild to wild. Use extreme discretion in choosing.

Would you rather...

be allowed to destroy Lego Land, pretending you are a giant monster
OR
be allowed to have a paintball war in the Vatican?

Would you rather always be...

16 **OR** 35?

12 **OR** 50?

2 **OR** 72?

Would you rather have sex with...

a virgin **OR** a porn star?

Jessicas Biel, Alba, and Simpson **OR** Jennifers Lopez, Garner, and Love Hewitt?

Wilma Flintstone **OR** Betty Rubble?

YOU MUST CHOOSE!

Would you rather have sex with...

George Clooney ten years ago **OR** Johnny Depp ten years from now?

a bad boy **OR** a choir boy?

Big Bird **OR** Megatron?

Would you rather...

watch a show called "The Biggest Luger"
OR
"Alzheimer's Patients Say the Darnedest Things"?

Would you rather spend a day with...

Terry Bradshaw **OR** Fred Armisen?

Al Franken **OR** Al Pacino?

Gary Gnu **OR** Will. I. Am?

YOU MUST CHOOSE!

Would you rather...

have an hour of conversation with Jesus

OR

an hour of wild sex with the celebrity of your choice?

Would you rather split a bottle of whiskey with...

Tommy Lee **OR** Stephen Hawking?

Howie Mandel **OR** Bilbo Baggins?

Malcolm X **OR** the Incredible Hulk?

Would you rather your partner...

compliment you

OR

complement you?

YOU MUST CHOOSE!

Would you rather...

smoke pot with Colin Powell

OR

Steven Spielberg?

Would you rather live in a world...

where humans engage in a jump ball to determine all disagreements

OR

where they play Rock Paper Scissors?

Would you rather...

be able to tap the phone of a celebrity of your choice

OR

an acquaintance of your choice?

YOU MUST CHOOSE!

Would you rather interview...

Thomas Edison **OR** Mother Teresa?

George Washington **OR** George Clooney?

a wasted Pat O'Brien **OR** a wasted Joe Namath?

Would you rather...

have a bowl of oatmeal with Charles Barkley

OR

dam a creek with Matt Lauer?

Would you rather...

catch crickets with Ben Kingsley

OR

construct a sofa fort with Michael Douglas?

YOU MUST CHOOSE!

Would you rather...

take a road trip with Socrates, Patrick Ewing, and Steve Carell

OR

your mom, Thomas Paine, and John Belushi?

Would you rather...

have Bobby Flay as your personal chef

OR

your choice of Angelina Jolie or Brad Pitt
as your personal sex slave?

Would you rather...

have phone sex with the banker from *Deal or No Deal*

OR

have "doodle sex" with the UPS commercial guy?

YOU MUST CHOOSE!

Would you rather...

LIVE IN A WORLD COMPOSED ENTIRELY OF NERF

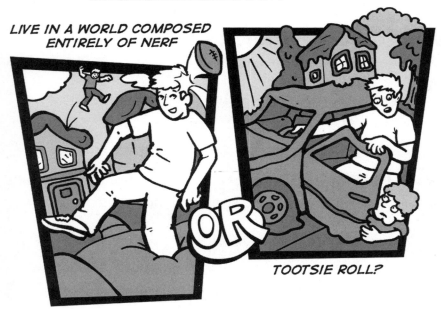

OR

TOOTSIE ROLL?

226

Would you rather...

get to be a guest judge on *American Idol*

OR

get to force one of your friends to go on it?

Would you rather...

have a comic book superhero based on you

OR

a reality show based on your life?

Things to consider: What would your powers be?

Would you rather...

have sex with Josh Duhamel and get genital warts

OR

have sex with Bryant Gumble and get a Louis Vuitton bag?

YOU MUST CHOOSE!

Would you rather...

have sex with Marissa Miller and get scurvy

OR

have sex with Joy Behar and get season tickets to your favorite football team?

Would you rather have sex with...

a 10 **OR** a 7 and a 3 at the same time?

ten 1's **OR** five 2's?

a 3, a 9, and a 1 **OR** a 4 and an 8?
Things to consider: Which bowling spare would you rather face?

Would you rather...

have a wise black caddy always hanging around to give you homespun advice

OR

have an unlimited supply of taffy?

YOU MUST CHOOSE!

Would you rather...

LIVE IN THE STAR TREK UNIVERSE

OR

THE WORLD OF DR. SEUSS?

Would you rather...

go to Vegas with Einstein

OR

Shakespeare?

Things to consider: card-counting, picking up chicks

Would you rather have it be...

Christmas every day **OR** Thanksgiving?

your wedding day **OR** a friend's wedding day?

a Bar-mitzvah **OR** Arbor Day?

Would you rather...

go to outer space

OR

have a threesome with two hot twins?

YOU MUST CHOOSE!

Would you rather...

have a staring contest with the Pope

OR

play ping pong against Kim Jong-il?

Would you rather...

have a street named after you

OR

have a martial art developed based on your physical style?
Things to consider: What would it be called, look like?

Would you rather...

be able to change a physical feature of yourself

OR

of your partner?

YOU MUST CHOOSE!

Would you rather have a bedroom designed by...

the people that make James Bond contraptions **OR** MC Escher?

Dr. Seuss **OR** Frank Lloyd Wright?

Would you rather...

have Ken Burns make a 14 part miniseries about your life full of low-key interviews and pan-dissolves

OR

have Michelangelo make a sculpture of you?

Would you rather...

be fluent in Latin

OR

Pig-Latin?

YOU MUST CHOOSE!

Would you rather have a different one-of-a-kind outfit designed for you every day by...

Christian Siriano **OR** Zac Posen?

Ralph Lauren **OR** Givenchy?

Dolce & Gabanna **OR** Stella McCartney?

Would you rather...

have lived the life of James Madison **OR** Wilt Chamberlain?

Paul McCartney **OR** Tiger Woods?

your mom **OR** your dad?

YOU MUST CHOOSE!

C H A P T E R   E L E V E N

WHAT WOULD YOU BE?
How to Use This Chapter

Game 1: *I Am Thinking of Someone We All Know.*

This is a way to use this chapter as a group game. One player thinks of someone who everybody in the group knows: a friend, a coworker, an enemy, a teacher, etc. This is the "name on the table." Other players take turns reading a randomly selected page of questions from this chapter. The player who is thinking of someone answers each question as if he were that person. After every page, have a player guess who you are thinking of. *Optional: If you want, you can all write down a bunch of people you know on scraps of paper, turn them over, and have the answerer pull a name from the pile.*

Game 2: *Conversation*.

Pretty simple. Read a question and answer it as yourself. If there is a group of you, everybody should answer the question. Suggest your own answers for what you think others are and discuss why. See who agrees and who disagrees. Debate. Deliberate. Arm-wrestle. Think about other people you know (your friends, family, bosses, etc.) and what they would be. When the conversation fades into silence and awkward stares—you guessed it—it's time to move on to the next question.

Game 3: *Celebrity*.

Go back a page. Reread the directions for Game 1, but substitute "celebrity" for "someone who everybody in the group knows."

Game 4: *Ninja Strike*.

Find a horde of bandits marauding caravans. Train in the martial arts, specializing in book warfare. Fashion this book into a throwing star or other deadly piece of weaponry. Defeat marauders.

If you were a **color,** what would you be?

If you were a **dog**, what breed would you be? What would your bark sound like?

If you were a *Simpsons character*, who would you be?

If you were a **type of car**, what make and model would you be? What condition are you in? How many miles do you have on you?

JAUNDICE

YOU MUST CHOOSE!

WHAT WOULD YOU BE?

If you were a punctuation mark, what would you be? A few to choose from: ? ! ; * , / ( ) $ & . and don't forget the versatile #, the smug ^ , or the wily ~

If you were a beat, what would you be? (Drum it or beatbox it.)

If you were a type of cheese, what would you be?

If you were a member of the A-Team, which character would you be?
Things to consider: Are you crazy? Are you slick and good-looking? Do you enjoy the culmination of a plan? Are you a large black man with a Mohawk who wears a preposterous amount of jewelry and has an aversion to air travel?

YOU MUST CHOOSE!

If you were a weather forecast, what would you be? Give the forecast as if a weatherman: For example, "Mostly sunny with a chance of afternoon thunderstorms. Some storms might be severe, becoming cooler at night..."

If you were a state, which would you be?

Things to consider: Are you dry? Hot? Do you have a panhandle?

If you were a Beatle, which one would you be?

If you were a tattoo, what would you be and on what part of the body?

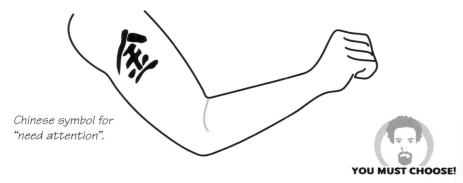

Chinese symbol for "need attention".

YOU MUST CHOOSE!

PHYSICAL PHUN!

If you were a facial expression, what would you be? (Make it.)

If you were a walk (a strut, a trot, an affected limp for sympathy, etc.), what would you be? (Walk it.)

If you were a sexual position, what would you be? (Demonstrate it with five thrusts. Use another person if need be.)

QUESTION OF CHARACTER

If you had to partake in sexual role-playing, what fantasy would appeal to you most: a) "Teacher Keeps Bookish Student after Class"; b) "Football Player Meets Cheerleader in Locker Room"; or c) "Post-Roast Beef Sandwich Consumption Run-in with Anonymous Thin Moroccan in Arby's Bathroom Stall"?

YOU MUST CHOOSE!

If you were a **font**, which would you be?

Serpentine

Tiki Surf

META - BOLD CAPS

Balzano

RUBBER STAMP

BOYCOTT

Jokerman

Cat Krap

Tekton Pro Bold

σψμβολ

Whimsy ICG

Funky Western

Interstate Hairline

Did you know?

The font that gets laid the most is *French Script*, while **Goudy Stout** is gay. **Bauhaus** and Lucida Sans Unicode are both virgins.

YOU MUST CHOOSE!

If you were a finger, which would you be (Pinky, Ring, Middle, Index, Thumb)?

If you were a movie genre, what would you be? What would your Motion Picture Association movie rating be? (G, PG, R, etc.)

If you were a city, which would you be?
Things to consider: Are you fast-paced? Laid-back? Do you have a giant arch protruding from you?

If you were a painting, what would you be? If you can't think of any, choose between *The Starry Night* by Vincent Van Gogh, a calm landscape scene of an ocean with a lighthouse, a wild and abstract Jackson Pollock splatter-painting, or *Dogs Playing Poker*.

YOU MUST CHOOSE!

For the following questions, use your cell phones or PDAs to answer.

If you were a **cell phone ring**, what would you be? Go through your phone's rings until you get the best one.

If you were a **type of cell phone** or **PDA** (iPhone, Blackberry, etc.), what would you be? What if you were a PDA as in public display of affection? (Demonstrate it.)

If you were a **text message using only 5 letters**, what would you be? (Text it.)

QUESTION OF CHARACTER

Who would be your ideal phone sex partner?
Some ideas: Angelina Jolie, Russell Crowe, Jenna Jameson, Lou Dobbs, Marcel Marceau, the *Inside the NFL* guy, Yourself.

YOU MUST CHOOSE!

Are you...

a **Mac** or **PC?**

a **Dog** or **Cat?**

Salt or **Pepper?**

Abbott or **Costello?**

Sugar or **Spice?**

Day or **Night?**

a **Beach** or **Mountain?**

Doo-doo or **Pee-pee?**

YOU MUST CHOOSE!

If you were a gem or precious stone, what would you be?

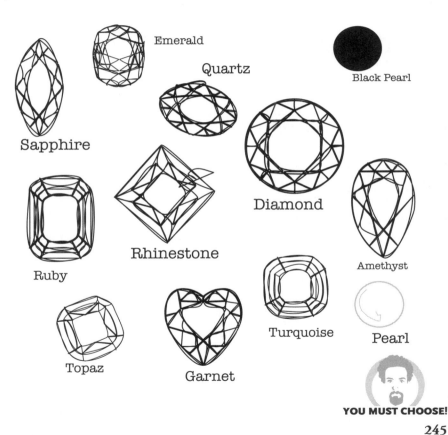

Emerald

Quartz

Black Pearl

Sapphire

Diamond

Ruby

Rhinestone

Amethyst

Topaz

Garnet

Turquoise

Pearl

YOU MUST CHOOSE!

YOU ARE WHAT YOU EAT!

If you were a bar drink or cocktail, what would you be?
Things to consider: Are you strong? Watered down? Fruity?

If you were a condiment, what would you be?

If you were a dessert, what would you be? What would the nutrition label say?

If you were a cereal, which would you be? How about if you were a cereal mascot?
Things to consider: Why are all cereal mascots either addicts or pushers?

YOU MUST CHOOSE!

If you were a **cartoon character**, who would you be?

If you were a **deodorant scent**, what would you be?
Things to consider: alpine frost, cool breeze, clean blast, tundratastic, salmon

If you were an **exclamation** or **sound made during sex**, what would you be? (Say it like you mean it!)

If you were an **onomatopoeia** (a sound-word like SMACK, THUD, SPLAT, or SQUISH), what would you be?
Things to consider: We hope your answer to this question was not the same as the answer to the previous question.

YOU MUST CHOOSE!

QUIZ 1

Who is this actor?

If he were an animal, he'd be a fox.

If he were an article of clothing, he'd be a tailored suit.

If he were a drink, he'd be a martini.

If he were a movie character, he'd be James Bond.

Answer: George Clooney

If you were any **character from a movie** or **TV show**, who would you be?

If you were a **part of the body**, what would you be?

If you were a **shape**, what would you be? (Draw it.)

If you were any **famous John**, which John would you be?
Things to consider: Do you have a macho Western air about you? Does sunshine on your shoulders make you happy? Do you have large genitals? Do you have mutilated genitals?

If you were a **famous Jen** or **Jennifer**, who would you be?

YOU MUST CHOOSE!

If you were a **speed limit**, what would you be?

If you were a **type of terrain** (mountains, desert, foothills, etc.), what would you be?

If you were a **piece of furniture**, what would you be?
Things to consider: Are you leather? Worn down? Modern? Classic?

If you were a **candy bar**, what would you be?

Did you know?

The Charleston Chew was invented by the Nazis as a battle snack.*

*Not true.

YOU MUST CHOOSE!

If you were a **musical instrument**, what would you be?

If you were a **musical note** or **chord**, what would you sound like? (Hum the note or play it if an instrument is near.)

Express who you are in a **drum solo**.

Express who you are by 20 seconds of **air guitar**.

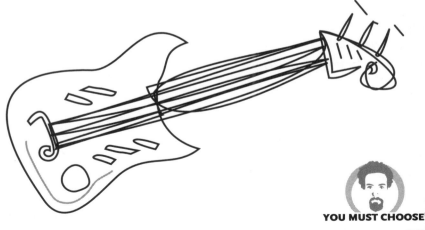

YOU MUST CHOOSE!

If you were a **zoo animal**, what would you be?

If you were a **circus act**, what would you be?

If you were **something in Australia**, what would you be?

If you were a **Greek god**, who would you be?

QUESTION OF CHARACTER

What would you want to be God of if you could be God of something? Fashion? Flatulence? Bad Hair Days? First Dates? Ennui?

YOU MUST CHOOSE!

GONE HOLLYWOOD

If you were a movie, what movie would you be?
Some ideas: When Harry Met Sally, Friday the 13th, Rocky,
Pulp Fiction, Big Breast Bangers 8, Big Breast Bangers 9.

If you were an actor/actress, who would you be?

If you were a Hollywood super couple, who
would you be?
Things to consider: TomKat, Brangelina, Bennifer, Fabioprah.

QUESTION OF CHARACTER

If your life were to get an Oscar nomination,
what would it be for? Best actor? Best supporting
actor? Best writing? Best score? Special effects?

YOU MUST CHOOSE!

If you were a **hairstyle**, what would you be?
Some (but not all) to choose from:

Crew cut
Says: All business.

Spiked Mohawk
Says: "F off."

Mullet
Says: Business in the front. Party in the back.

The Visor
Says: Party in the front. Business in the back.

The Afro
Says: Party everywhere.

Pony tail.
Says: (for women) – **I'm playful and energetic.** (for men) – **I'm sensitive and trying to get laid.**

The Anchorman
Says: **That shouldn't be a problem.**

Middle part
Says: **Precision, symmetry. 1983.**

Jheri Curls
Says: **It all.**

YOU MUST CHOOSE!

If you were a **month**, what would you be?

If you were a **playing card**, what would you be?

If you were a **country**, what would you be?

If you were a **sound**, what would you be?
Things to consider: a foghorn, a last gasp, glass breaking, wind chimes, gong

256

YOU MUST CHOOSE!

ORIGA-ME

Tear this page out and make an **origami** (folded paper sculpture) that represents you.

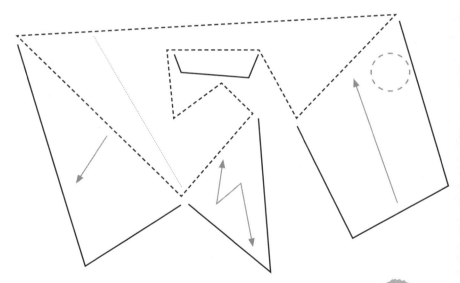

YOU MUST CHOOSE!

ANIMAL INSTINCTS

If you were a creature of the sea, what would you be?

If you were a mammal, what would you be?

If you were an insect, what would you be?

If you were a bird, what would you be?

If you could create an animal that was you, what would it be?

Head of a _____? Body of a _____?

Hands/claws of a_____ ? Mind of a _____?

Courage of a _____?

YOU MUST CHOOSE!

Are you…

a **fork**, **knife**, or **spoon**?

rock, **paper**, or **scissors**?

a **red**, **yellow**, or **green light**?

a **yes**, **no**, or **maybe**?

Larry, **Curly**, or **Moe**?

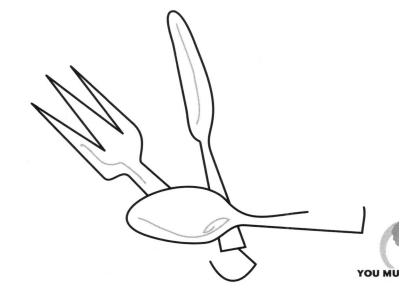

YOU MUST CHOOSE!

If you were a song, what song would you be? Which rendition? (Sing it.)

If you were a spice, what would you be?

If you were a Spice Girl, which would you be?

If you were a famous historical figure, who would you be?

Did you know?

Confederacy President Jefferson Davis invented the high five.*

*Not true.

YOU MUST CHOOSE!

If you were a **hand tool**, what would you be?

If you were a **flower** or **plant**, what would you be?

If you were a **character in the Bible**, which would you be?

If you were a **video game character**, what character would you be?

QUESTION OF CHARACTER

What if you were a **character in a video game based on the Bible?** How would the game go? You get points for all the lepers you heal? All the suffering you can bear? All the outdated passages you interpret literally?

YOU MUST CHOOSE!

261

YOU ARE WHAT YOU WRITE

If you were handwriting, what would you be? Write a sentence in the handwriting that captures your essence.

If you were a work of abstract art, what would you be? (Draw it.)

If you were an Instant Message acronym (LOL, BRB, TTYL, etc.), what would you be?

IM acronyms for super villains: MLOL (Maniacal laugh out loud); IWDY (I will destroy you); (BRBBYW) (Be right back, but you won't); ISSATEIAFIRFIWAANWIMOIE (I shall sweep away the Earth in a fiery inferno, recreating from its windblown ashes a new world in my own image everlasting)

YOU MUST CHOOSE!

262

If you were a planet, which one would you be?
Things to consider: the beauty and mystique of Saturn, Jupiter the gas giant, the tempestuous and hot Venus, Uranus.

If you were a metal, what would you be?
Things to consider: Are you strong? Lustrous? Precious?

If you were a curse word, what would you be? How would you be said? (Demonstrate.)

If you were a monster, what would you be?
Things to consider: vampire, zombie, yeti, black pudding, pubic elves, (See "About the Author" for the monster called Gomberg).

Ringed Planets

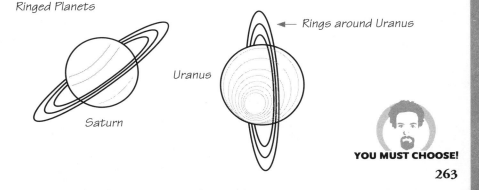

Rings around Uranus

Uranus

Saturn

YOU MUST CHOOSE!

QUIZ 2

Who is this celebrity?

If he were a food, he'd be cheese.

If he were a color, he'd be gold.

If he were a playing card, he'd be the Ace of Spades.

If he were a character from a movie, he'd be Gordon Gekko.

Answer: Donald Trump

If you were a **Smurf**, who would you be?

If you were **one of the seven dwarves**, which would you be?

If you were **one of the symptoms Nyquil is meant to help with**, which would you be?

If you were a **kickball pitch** ("slow and smooth", "fast and bouncy", etc.), what would you be?

Ambivalent Smurf

YOU MUST CHOOSE!

265

If you were a time of the day, what would you be?

If you were any character from a book, who would you be?

Things to consider: Holden Caulfield, Frodo Baggins, Scout, Encyclopedia Brown, Hamlet, Flat Stanley

If you were a type of building (hut, skyscraper, wigwam, office park), what would you be?

If you were a comic strip character, who would you be?

Things to consider: Dilbert, Garfield, Prince Valiant, Calvin, a Far Side cow, the Would You Rather...? guy (see the book Would You Rather...? Illustrated).

QUESTION OF CHARACTER

If you had a vanity plate on your car, what would you have? (Examples: IMCOOL, WADEVA, 2MUCH, ILUVSOD, etc.)

YOU MUST CHOOSE!

Which one of you...

Which one of you or your friends is **Q*bert**?

Which one of you or your friends is a **desert**?

Which one of you or your friends is a **ruby**?

Which one of you or your friends is **The Fonz**?

Which one of you or your friends is **Swing dance**?

If you were a **book genre**, what would you be?

If you were a **morning beverage**, what would you be?

If you were **one of the founding fathers**,
who would you be?

Things to consider: the quiet but brilliant James Madison; the inflexible but eloquent Jefferson, the bold and commanding Washington, the bloated and problem-flatulent Templeton.

Did you know?

The reason John Hancock signed his name larger than normal on the Declaration of Independence is because he had hands twice the size of a normal human being.*

*Not true. The real reason he signed so big was because he was an asshole.

YOU MUST CHOOSE!

LIFE'S A GAMBLE

If you were a **casino game**, what would you be?

How about if you were a **blackjack hand**?

A poker hand?

A roll of the dice in craps?

And finally, **finish this slot machine spin**:
Cherry... Cherry... and...

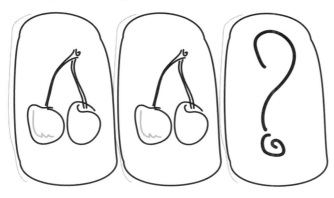

YOU MUST CHOOSE!

WHAT WOULD YOU BE?

QUESTION OF CHARACTER

What's in a Name?

Choose a **name** that best expresses your essence:

If you had a **rapper name**, what would it be?

If you had a **porn star name**, what would it be?

If you had a **pirate name**, what would it be?

If you had a *Dungeons & Dragons* name, what would it be?

If you had a **Mafia name**, what would it be?

YOU MUST CHOOSE!

If you were a **type of vehicle**, what would you be?

If you were a **street in New York City**, what would you be? Describe it in detail.
Things to consider: Wall Street, Park Avenue, a street in the West Village, a Harlem alley.

If you were a **famous landmark**, what would you be?

If you were a **smell**, what would you be?
Things to consider: roses, suntan oil, mulch, tar, new sheets, ass, BBQ, all of the above.

YOU MUST CHOOSE!

CHAPTER TWELVE

EXTREME BEAUTY, BODY, APPEARANCE AND FASHION

Gone are the days where dying your hair blue made you extreme.
That's downright conformist these days. To be avant-garde now means
piercing your nose with a chain connected to a live mallard or getting
a full body tattoo of an elk raping a walrus. With these new standards
of extreme in mind, we present to you some choices in forward-thinking
fashion and bodywork.

Would you rather...

get a face lift on only the left side of your face

OR

inject your eyelids with two pounds of collagen?

Things to consider: looking/talking like Rocky

Would you rather...

have a migrating mole beauty mark that wanders all over your face

OR

have 8-balls for pupils?

Would you rather...

be limited to wearing Tevas and socks for footwear

OR

only be able to use a plastic Walgreen's bag as a purse or wallet?

YOU MUST CHOOSE!

Would you rather...

have to wear a Snuggie in public every day

OR

have to wear a matching terrycloth headband and wristbands?

Would you rather...

have noses protruding from all over your body

OR

have 6 foot long armpit hair?

Would you rather...

all your weight go to your thighs **OR** to your butt?

to your stomach **OR** to your ankles and upper arms?

to your neck **OR** to your forehead?

YOU MUST CHOOSE!

Would you rather...

have perpetual camel toe

OR

perpetual muffin-top?

Would you rather...

be limited to a half pound of clothing every day

OR

have to wear no less than 30 pounds of jewelry?

Things to consider: exercising at the gym, cold days

Would you rather...

have broccoli for hair **OR** pins for facial hair?

ladles for hands **OR** large dreidels for feet?

a live sparrow for a belly button **OR** pumpkins for testicles?

YOU MUST CHOOSE!

Would you rather...

be on *Project Runway*

OR

have your significant other go on *What Not to Wear*?

Would you rather...

have eyelashes that connect from one eye to the other

OR

nose hair that connects from one nostril to the other?

Would you rather...

receive every haircut from a non-English speaking stylist at Supercuts

OR

have your wardrobe consist exclusively of Dress Barn hand-me-downs?

YOU MUST CHOOSE!

Would you rather...

have copious amounts of areola hair

OR

a "happy trail" that reached your neck?

Would you rather...

have to wear a four pound nipple piercing

OR

have a four-inch radius genital hoop ring?

Would you...

pay an additional 20% income tax for the rest of your life if you could give all your weight-gain to another person of your choosing?

YOU MUST CHOOSE!

SPA MENU

The Deity invites you to enjoy a spa weekend. He hands you an itinerary and firmly reminds you the choices are mandatory.

Would you rather take...

a sewage mudbath

OR

a human sweat Jacuzzi?

Would you rather...

get a whale sperm facial

OR

Magic Shell microdermabrasion?

YOU MUST CHOOSE!

Would you rather...

have to wear live spider earrings

OR

used tampon earrings?

Would you rather...

have to always go shopping and try on clothes with your mother

OR

have to go shopping and try on clothes with an invective-spitting Stacy and Clinton from *What Not To Wear?*

Would you rather...

always wear a top that left two holes for your nipples

OR

a pair of spandex with an ambiguous misshapen bulge at your crotch?

YOU MUST CHOOSE!

Would you rather...

have your arms come out of your head

OR

come out of your knees?

Would you rather...

have a barely formed second head of Bob Barker sprouting from the side of your own head

OR

have your head permanently turned 45 degrees?

Would you rather...

have a goatee around each eye

OR

earlobes that connected under your chin?

YOU MUST CHOOSE!

Would you rather...

have extra eyeballs in the palms of your hands

OR

have hair that styles itself?

Would you rather...

the current fashion trend be high-waisted jeans

OR

low-waisted?

Would you rather...

only wear clothes on the left side of your body

OR

only on the bottom half?

YOU MUST CHOOSE!

Would you rather...

shave your pubic area in a question mark

OR

exclamation mark?

Things to consider: Which one symbolizes that area better?

Would you rather always have to wear...

suspenders adorned with no less than 15 pieces of flair **OR** a tiara?

a marching band's drum on your shoulders **OR** orthodontic headgear?

a solid gold grill over your teeth **OR** 14 tubes of lipstick (you can use it wherever as long as it is exposed)?

Would you rather...

have to heavily bedazzle every article of clothing you own

OR

whenever outside, have to wear sunglasses in which each lens is as large as your head?

YOU MUST CHOOSE!

Would you rather...

have tempura-battered nipples

OR

produce caramel under your arms when sweating?

Would you rather...

have the physique of Gollum from *Lord of the Rings*

OR

Fat Albert?

Would you rather...

have the neck of a 90 year-old

OR

have the feet of a 90 year-old?

YOU MUST CHOOSE!

Would you rather...

have perpetually lit candle wicks at the end of each finger

OR

have sixteen-knuckled fingers?

Would you rather...

have to wear a nose ring that is connected to an earring with only a two inch chain

OR

have to wear a lip ring connected to a belly button ring with a twelve inch chain?

Would you rather...

have to wear three layers of sweats whenever you go to the beach

OR

wear Borat's neon green stretchy one-piece bathing suit whenever you go to the beach?

YOU MUST CHOOSE!

285

Would you rather...

have cellulite over 100% of your body

OR

have smooth skin but weigh 300 pounds?

Would you rather...

have Meg Ryan's cosmetic surgeon

OR

Kenny Rogers' cosmetic surgeon?

Would you rather...

gain 30 pounds

OR

three pounds all in your face?

YOU MUST CHOOSE!

Would you rather...

wear cologne scented as hot tar

OR

fish taco?

Would you rather...

have your eyes and big toes switch places

OR

your nose and belly button?

Would you rather...

have skin that rusts but never wrinkles

OR

have hair that doesn't gray but begins to stop responding to gravity?

YOU MUST CHOOSE!

Would you rather always have to wear...

knee pads **OR** elbow pads?

an Eskimo coat **OR** a T-shirt that says "Makin' Bacon" along with a picture of two pigs humping?

a salami eye patch **OR** a lettuce yarmulke?

Would you rather...

have razor burn that forms treasure maps

OR

acne that spells out Braille love poetry?
Things to consider: marrying a blind person

Would you rather...

drool creamed spinach

OR

lactate Tang?

YOU MUST CHOOSE!

Would you rather...

HAVE A COMB-OVER FROM YOUR EYEBROWS

OR

FROM YOUR BACKHAIR?

Would you rather...

have stretch marks all over your face

OR

have a pimento in each ear?

Would you rather...

have Patrick Ewing's arms on your body

OR

Patrick Ewing's nose on your face?

Would you rather...

have constantly wriggling body hair

OR

have a mustache that is constantly doing the wave?

YOU MUST CHOOSE!

Would you rather...

HAVE TATTOOS OF VARIOUS GEOMETRIC FORMULAS

OR

ALL OF THE US VICE PRESIDENTS' HEADS?

Would you rather...

have a head that is half normal size

OR

twice normal size?

Would you rather...

fart the smell of lavender

OR

belch the sound of church bells in the distance?

Would you rather...

allow your mom to pick a tattoo for you

OR

allow your sibling?

YOU MUST CHOOSE!

Would you rather wear clothes made of...

balsa wood **OR** Fruit Roll-Up?

bamboo **OR** tin foil?

old '80s album covers **OR** Atari boxes?

Would you rather...

have nostrils that are constantly blowing out air

OR

a navel that is constantly sucking in air?

YOU MUST CHOOSE!

AUTHORS' DEBATE

AUTHORS' DEBATE

Let me proceed — Justin Heimberg

All it takes is some smart attentive constant grooming, and you'll look perfectly normal. If you're feeling lazy, you can just let it grow and swoosh it to the side like that Blagojevich guy. You can even cultivate the Travolta-like widow's peak with some artful shaving. A receding hairline gives you no choice other than go bald or a front-comb, the most perverse of the comb-over's incarnations. There's no freedom in that. In today's economy, you need to be recession-proof.

Let me recede — David Gomberg

Thanks to Michael Jordan, baldness became an acceptable even chic hairstyle—for black people in the '80s, and for white people a short fifteen years later. You can always shave your head close when it becomes too thin and scraggly. And you know where you're headed with male pattern baldness. But where does the hair procession stop? Does it sneak down your nose, over your lips, dribbling down your chin and neck, extending into a hairy isthmus[1] merging with your pubes? And yes, you can shave this torrent of hair, but then you need to deal with forehead stubble, which while a great band name, is a hideous and grotesque image.

1 And A Happy New Year!

CHAPTER THIRTEEN

EXTREMELY PERSONAL

It's time to get personal. How personal? We'll give you a hint. It rhymes with "blexcreamley". It's not hard. Just personalize WYR by taking the everyday people in your life and placing them in the following extreme situations.

Would you rather...

give a feverish lap dance to _____
(insert friend's mom)

OR

get a feverish lap dance from _____ ?
(insert another friend's mom)

Would you rather...

fight _____
(insert tough acquaintance)

OR

have sex with _____ ?
(insert gross acquaintance)

Would you...

passionately kiss _____ to have sex with _____ ?
(insert relative) (insert someone hot)

YOU MUST CHOOSE!

Would you rather...

have the person on your left's hair

OR

the person on your right's butt?

Would you rather...

bump, grind, freak, and otherwise dirty dance
with _____
(insert friend's mom or teacher or someone else inappropriate)

OR

pose naked for _____ ?
(insert magazine)

Would you rather...

forcefully punch _____ in the _____
(insert relative)   (insert body part)

OR

smother and kill _____ ?
(insert pet)

YOU MUST CHOOSE!

Would you rather...

have _____'s body
(insert fit friend)

OR

_____'s intelligence?
(insert smart friend)

Would you rather...

have a threesome with _____
and _____
(insert attractive acquaintance)
(insert unattractive acquaintance)

OR

have a threesome with _____ ?
(insert two average looking acquaintances)

Would you rather...

be Siamese twins with _____
(insert disgusting acquaintance)

OR

_____ ?
(insert annoying acquaintance)

YOU MUST CHOOSE!

Would you rather...

have a Real Doll of _____
(insert someone you know)

OR

a voodoo doll of _____ ?
(insert someone you dislike)

Would you rather...

have _____ 's clothes
(insert unstylish person)

OR

_____ 's imagination?
(insert boring person)

Would you rather...

grope _____
(insert hot person)

OR

have sex with _____ ?
(insert average looking person)

YOU MUST CHOOSE!

Would you rather...

fight in the octagon _____
(insert bad-ass acquaintance)

OR

four _____ s?
(insert wimpy acquaintance)

Would you rather...

be stuck on a desert island with your parents

OR

_____ ?
(insert somewhat unappealing person)

Would you rather...

fart wetly and loudly in front of _____
(insert relative)

OR

_____ ?
(insert someone you have a crush on or are trying to impress)

Would you rather...

club _____
(insert baby animal)

OR

go clubbing with _____ ?
(insert worst person you know)

YOU MUST CHOOSE!

Would you rather...

take a clean punch to the jaw by _____
(insert strong friend)

OR

spend a sixteen hour car ride with _____ ?
(insert annoying person)

Would you rather...

have _____ 's nose
(insert someone you are with)

OR

_____ 's body?
(insert someone else you are with)

Would you rather...

believe in the philosophical views of _____
(insert philosopher)

OR

_____ ?
(insert five year-old you know)

YOU MUST CHOOSE!

Would you rather...

take off your clothes, squat, and make a number two
in front of _____
(insert friend's parents)

OR

put a mask on, sneak up, and put a sleeper hold
on _____ ?
(insert friend's mom)

If your life depended on it,
would you rather...

have _____ as your tennis partner
(insert uncoordinated friend)

OR

_____ as your partner on *Password*?
(insert dumb acquaintance)

Would you rather...

have your genitals located on your _____
(insert body part)

OR

your _____ ?
(insert another body part)

YOU MUST CHOOSE!

Would you rather...

have to mutually masturbate with _____

(insert inappropriate acquaintance)

OR

go down on _____ ?

(insert unhygienic person)

Would you rather...

make pancakes with _____

(insert random person)

OR

play Wiffleball with _____ ?

(insert another random person)

Would you rather...

drop your pants and moon _____

(insert relative)

OR

give a hickey to _____ ?

(insert disgusting person)

YOU MUST CHOOSE!

Would you rather...

spend one week handcuffed to _____
(insert most shy acquaintance)

OR

_____ ?
(insert most garrulous acquaintance)

Would you rather...

cc _____ on all of your emails for a week
(insert someone else's parents)

OR

have _____ have access to your Internet browser history?
(insert dignified acquaintance)

Would you rather...

suck the toes of _____
(insert most vile acquaintance)

OR

vigorously tongue the armpits of _____ ?
(insert least hygienic friend)

YOU MUST CHOOSE!

Would you rather...

push _____ in front of a moving vehicle
        (insert close friend)

OR

play one round of Russian roulette with _____ ?
                                            (insert member of immediate family)

Would you rather...

manually stimulate _____
                        (insert close friend's father)

OR

have a three-way with _____ while _____
                        (insert close friend's parents)   (insert the ghost of a historical figure)
watched?

Would you rather...

have nightly sex with _____ for a week
                            (insert unattractive person)

OR

for the same week, be the official "wiper"
of _____ ?
        (insert person you know with worst stomach issues)

YOU MUST CHOOSE!

EXTREMELY PERSONAL

CHAPTER FOURTEEN

14

WOULD YOU...

Simple yes or no questions aren't always so simple. For example, "Examined within a framework of dialectal materialism, was Marx right when he professed that those who control the means of production inevitably usurp power from the bourgeois?" Luckily for you, only a few of the following "Would you...?" questions concern dialectical materialism, and even those in some way tend to involve farting.

Would you...

spend two weeks wearing nothing but a g-string and Tevas for $20,000?

Would you...

sit in the bleachers and heckle the outfielders at a Special Olympics softball game for an inning for $13,000?

Would you...

take the surname of your spouse upon marriage (they were adamant about it) if it were "Chode"? "Doodition"? Cheeksqueakers?"

Would you...

pay $10,000 a year for a personal blues musician who magically appears to give harmonica accompaniment when you start complaining?

YOU MUST CHOOSE!

Would you...
masturbate only to *National Geographic* for the rest of your life for $500,000?

Would you...
change your name to "Blelko McGubbern" for $200,000?

Would you...
anonymously, wearing a mask, kick your grandma in the stomach for $100,000?

Then would you knee her jaw for $600,000?

Then spear her to the ground for $300,000?

Then blow a snot-rocket on her for $75,000?

Then drop a big elbow on her for $200,000 — totaling $1,275,000?

YOU MUST CHOOSE!

Would you...

accept the power to be able to fly in exchange for weighing 500 pounds?

Would you...

attempt to hold in your bowel movements for two weeks for $50,000 if and only if you succeed?

Would you...

have your nose surgically altered so that you have one giant nostril for $3,000,000?

YOU MUST CHOOSE!

If you never got caught, would you...

cheat on your partner with your choice of George Clooney or Jessica Alba?

If you never got caught, would you...

cheat on your partner with your choice all of the Victoria's Secret models at once or your top five rock stars?

YOU MUST CHOOSE!

For $300,000 deposited in your bank account today, would you name your kid...

Scrotie?

Rommel?

Neldar 9?

DeJustin?

Porp-Porp?

The sound of a bus door opening?

Would you...

wear a monocle to your job for a day for $500?

YOU MUST CHOOSE!

Would you...

if the Deity made it possible, have a third nipple for $100,000?
At $100,000 a nipple, how many would you have?

Would you...

get a large back tattoo of Andy Griffith for $20,000?

Would you, if there were no consequences...

slap Paula Abdul in the face?

Would you, if there were no consequences...

punch Donald Trump in the face?

YOU MUST CHOOSE!

Would you...

adopt your partner's hairstyle for $25,000 a year as long as you kept it?

Would you...

have sex with a baby harp seal to have sex with all the Playmates of the current year (men); with *People's 50 Sexiest Men* (women)?

Would you...

attempt to remove your own appendix with a pocket knife and some rubbing alcohol for $5,000,000?

Would you...

step in front of an 8 year-old to catch a foul ball at a baseball game if you knew you'd catch it?

YOU MUST CHOOSE!

WINNER TAKES HOME $1,000,000, AND THE FIGHT IS TO THE DEATH.

Would you fight...

two emus?

Prince, if he had a knife?

600 tortoises?

a samurai who is on his cell phone possibly breaking up with his girlfriend?

1,000 possessed paper clips?

Would you...

permanently lose ten IQ points if you lost ten pounds permanently?

YOU MUST CHOOSE!

Would you...

wear swim goggles all week for $1,000?
Make it happen.

Would you...

sit on a bowl of green beans for an hour for $120 dollars?
Make it happen.

Would you...

want your partner to permanently lose ten IQ points if they lost
ten pounds permanently?

Would you...

offer advertising on your gravestone if it gave those mentioned
in your will $1,000 a month increasing at the rate of inflation?

YOU MUST CHOOSE!

Would you...

stoop to using the homeless holding signs advertising your business if you could pay them only a dollar a day?

Would you...

put product placement in your every day dialogue (have to mention, say, Kellog's cereals at least 40 times a day in your every day conversations) for $100 a day? Example: "The day is as nice as Special K is crunchy! How are the kids?"

Would you...

want to have sex with Jennifer Lopez if she gained 50 pounds? 80? 100? 200?

Would you...

want to have sex with Johnny Depp if he gained 50 pounds? 100? 200?

YOU MUST CHOOSE!

Would you...

for $3,000, go to a junior high school, wait outside, and then when a nerdy kid walks out, walk past him and knock his books down in front of everybody, then walk away, never to be seen again?

Would you...

blog about your relationship life for $1,000 a week?

Would you...

pay $2,000 a year for a personal clothes shopper for your partner?

Would you...

fight a retarded cougar to the death if the winner gets $1,000,000?

YOU MUST CHOOSE!

Would you...

have sex with Leonard DiCaprio (women)/Shakira (men) if he/she had no teeth? No teeth and no hair? No teeth, no hair, no knees, and an incurable case of the hiccups?

Would you...

type left-handed for the rest of your life if you could have unlimited sex with any porn star you wanted? Would you type with your tongue for the rest of your life? With your genitals?

Would you...

lose a finger to have sex with your choice of Halle Berry or Tom Brady? A thumb? A hand? An arm? A leg?

Would you...

have a sex change operation for $20,000,000?

YOU MUST CHOOSE!

Would you...

limit your attire to various matador outfits for $500,000?

Would you...

put your penis in a glory hole for $60,000 if you were told there was an equal chance of your mother, Jenna Jameson, and Greg Gumbel being on the other side?

Would you...

watch a porno movie starring your parents for $1,000? $10,000? $100,000? What's your price?

Would you...

watch a porno movie with your parents for $1,000? $10,000? $100,000?

YOU MUST CHOOSE!

Which of the following would you have sex with for your choice of $200,000 or the chance to have sex with your "top five" selections for the people in the world you most want to have sex with?

A sheep?

A cow?

An armadillo?

A rhino?

Will Purdue?

A Winnie the Pooh hand puppet?

A baboon?

A pack of Ewoks?

YOU MUST CHOOSE!

323

Would you...

have sex with a creature that was half Lucy Liu/half horse?
Which half would you want as the lower half and which as the upper?

Would you slyly masturbate to the point of orgasm...

On a public bus for $5,000?

At a Quizno's for $7,000

At your desk at work during working hours for $10,000?

At church for $200,000?

YOU MUST CHOOSE!

Would you...

become a crack addict for one year if you were given $5,000,000 one month into your addiction? What if you were given the money after you completed your year?

Would you...

be defenestrated from a second story window for $8,000?

Would you...

be fenestrated into a first story window for $50?

Wludo ouy...

eb ldixscde orf ?005,00$.

YOU MUST CHOOSE!

EXTRA EXTREMELY EXTREME EXTRAS:

Would You Rather...?'s MindF*cks: 9 Things To Do in Airports to Screw with People's Heads

① Happily walk toward the metal detector. Scream in agony and convulse as you pass through it. Shoot a fearful look to the person behind you before hurrying off in a glazed shock.

② Get in a quick workout by running the opposite way on moving sidewalk. Wear a headband and spandex.

③ Bring individual grocery items including vegetables, deli meat, and hygiene products, and place them on the x-ray conveyor belt. Have your check book and supermarket club card out and ready.

④ Wrap a luggage tag around your wrist and ride the baggage carousel motionless.

⑤ Try to check in your luggage: a) one marble b) a horseshoe crab with a red ribbon around it c) an 8" by 10" photo of Konstantin Chernenko.

YOU MUST CHOOSE!

326

⑥ Fill Sudoku grids in the Air Flight magazine with the number 6 over and over.

⑦ At arrival area, hold up a sign that says Zarkon, Galactic Time Traveler of the Year 3000. Wear a silver foil vest and matching arm bands.

⑧ At metal detector, along with your keys and coins, put the following in trays: a dozen condoms, Mapquest directions to a church, and anal beads.

⑨ Check a Commodore 64 instead of a laptop through the carry-on x-ray.

YOU MUST CHOOSE!

CHAPTER FIFTEEN

EXTREMELY RANDOM

Before it was co-opted by the masses, *Would You Rather...?* was originally concocted for fans of "random" humor. In the spirit of the extreme, we venture back to our random roots. Be forewarned: you'll either love or hate this chapter. Or both. (Please send all love and/or hate mail to random@sevenfooter.com.)

Would you rather live in a world where...

people aged to age forty then reversed the aging process to their birth/death

OR

people didn't die, they rather gradually turned into celery?

Would you rather...

sweat profusely between the hours of six pm and seven pm

OR

insistently think your name is Darryl during the month of February?

Would you rather...

be able to catalyze enthusiastic low-fives from everybody you meet

OR

have a sixth sense which makes you tingle when in the presence of mechanical engineers?

YOU MUST CHOOSE!

Would you rather...

be able to multiply shinguards

OR

be able to correctly predict the date of any beaver's death?

Things to consider: See if you can come up with an even more useless power; email it to uselesspower@sevenfooter.com

Would you rather...

have a sarcastic echo that repeats whatever you say in a mocking inflection

OR

cast a shadow that's not your own, but rather that of Tennessee Williams?

Would you rather...

have a 200 IQ but have difficulty "using your words" like a two year-old

OR

have a darling figure but be morbidly obsessed with dandelions?

YOU MUST CHOOSE!

Would you rather...

have a literally contagious laugh that causes other people to laugh just like you

OR

be compelled to "spot" people and psych them up when they're picking luggage off the carousel at an airport?

If you could travel through time, would you rather...

play paddy-cake with Chiang Kai-shek

OR

play peek-a-boo with Bing Crosby?

Would you rather...

have to stick every piece of gum you ever chew somewhere on your body when you're done with it

OR

always be blowing your breath hard and making an intense grimacing face like a dude bench-pressing?

YOU MUST CHOOSE!

Would you rather...

look like this

OR

look like this?

YOU MUST CHOOSE!

WOULD YOU RATHER...? FOR BEGINNERS

Would you rather...

be wealthy and happy

OR

be poor and malnourished?

Would you rather...

have high attractive angular cheek bones

OR

have an extremely lazy eye and cleft lip?

Would you rather...

have a delicate grace about you

OR

limp badly and have a club foot?

YOU MUST CHOOSE!

Would you rather...

marry a beautiful kind person

OR

a hideous, moronic jerk who plays the flute often, loudly, and badly?

Would you rather...

fight a creature with the head of a tiger and the body
of an anaconda

OR

a creature with the head of a trout and the body of a wallet?

YOU MUST CHOOSE!

Would you rather...

be bitten by a mosquito every ten seconds

OR

be bitten by former NBA great Ralph Sampson every two hours?

Would you rather...

have the stock ticker tape thing scrolling through your eyes
(you can still see)

OR

vehemently displace all your anger on a shy, undeserving busboy
named Luis?

YOU MUST CHOOSE!

Would you rather...

be incredibly sensitive to people named Melvin but have a blurry right ear

OR

only need three hours sleep but be allergic to anything purple?

Would you rather...

have a nasal condition whereupon blowing your nose, the Mormon Tabernacle Choir's chorus of "Hallelujah" rings out

OR

have your first-born come out looking exactly like a miniature Tony Bennet?

Would you rather...

have the voice in your head sound like Don Knotts

OR

have your self-esteem dependent upon your proximity to a Long John Silver's?

YOU MUST CHOOSE!

Would you rather...

HAVE SWISS CHEESE LINENS

OR

WALL TO WALL
GROUND BEEF CARPET?

Would you rather...

have flounder for a tongue

OR

a spatula for your left foot?

Would you rather...

be moisturized to death

OR

starve to death in your shower, unable to circumvent the lather/rinse/repeat conundrum?

Would you rather live in a world...

where the traditional greeting was to roll up your shirt, slap your stomach repeatedly and bellow "Baboosk!"

OR

where celebrities offered stool samples instead of autographs?

YOU MUST CHOOSE!

WOULD YOU LATHER...

(What began as a Japanese man's mispronunciation
became a game unto itself)

Would you lather... a Rottweiler?

Would you lather... Pat Sajak?

Would you lather... your naked self on national
TV for $50,000?

Would you lather... John Stamos's head circa 1985?

Would you rather...

have your sole pick-up line be "The Higgs Field is a theoretical superforce that permeates the universe endowing matter with mass"

OR

be forced to use only one perfume/cologne scent: bacon and herb?

Would you rather...

be reincarnated as an incontinent spaniel

OR

a bipolar frog?

Would you rather...

on Thursdays, become convinced that everybody's name is Stottlemeyer

OR

have an irresistible temptation to defecate in people's grandfather clocks?

YOU MUST CHOOSE!

Would you rather...

have a consistent long-range jumper but laugh hysterically at the sight of cream cheese?

OR

be extremely well-spoken but turn into McDonald's Grimace when the moon is full?

Would you rather...

bloppers dalst nork serstel rackel endo melp azoo

OR

ferden rappo lacas delden sasty moln, restee eisenclost zand?
Things to consider: Norbins, rastor clousers.

Would you rather...

have blood that smells like vanilla extract but have one of Mussolini's speeches boom from your hand whenever it was opened

OR

have perfect diction but compulsively hoard radishes, fondling them and giggling maniacally in their presence?

YOU MUST CHOOSE!

343

Would you rather...

have these stats:

 Str: 18

 Dex: 17

 Con: 4

 Int: 5

 Wis: 4

 Cha: 17

OR

these:

 Str: 5

 Dex: 4

 Con: 18

 Int: 17

 Wis: 18

 Cha: 4?

YOU MUST CHOOSE!

Would you rather be unable to distinguish between...

your shoes and milk cartons **OR** swabs and your keys?

the phrase "I love you" and the phrase "Pass the salt" **OR** the phrases "How are you?" and "I will destroy you!"?

the concept of reciprocity and coon-skin hats **OR** water and ballet?

Would you rather...

have extraordinary balance but have to wear a retainer the rest of your life

OR

have nifty word-smithing talent but have a pathological phobia of cummerbunds?

YOU MUST CHOOSE!

Would you rather...

have a dominating net game in tennis but be incapable
of recognizing the numeral 4

OR

be able to calculate exact postage for a letter/package by sight
but always have to keep your pubic hair gelled in Jheri curl style?

Would you rather...

be the spitting image of Sidney Poitier, but have calves as thick
as your waist

OR

be unbeatable when you throw first in backgammon,
but have frictionless soles on your feet?

Would you rather...

play dodgeball with Britain's House of Commons

OR

play Spud with the cast of Mr. Belvedere?

YOU MUST CHOOSE!

Would you rather...

jump on a grenade to save your friends and family

OR

just kind of slowly cover up the grenade?

Would you rather...

there was a silent "b" in "felt"

OR

the word "flounder" was spelled "pilfcone"?

Would you rather...

have the bunion of Paul Simon

OR

the Simon of Paul Bunyan (work in progress)?

EXTREMELY RANDOM

YOU MUST CHOOSE!

Would you rather...

have the navigational instincts of Amerigo Vespucci but subsist on a diet of pet food

OR

be able to shine shoes with your gaze but have to make love to a croissant on a daily basis?

YOU MUST CHOOSE!

Would you rather... have to walk single file with your friends whenever you went anywhere, have your dreams directed by the guy who directed Pan's Labyrinth, be able to enter the water without making a splash, but uncontrollably exclaim names of the various members of the Continental Congress during sexual climax

OR

have literal cauliflower ear, have a herring for a left hand, have to name your child Aesop, constantly be framing shots with your hands like a director, turn guys named Mervin yellow, and be able to spit pools that show visions of the future for a peasant in Laos?

YOU MUST CHOOSE!

Would you rather...

have a cork back, a comb-over beard, lust after Puss in Boots, have Wes Unseld's shadow, play daily *Arkanoid* games with Tony Randall, have to *register for your wedding* at Spencers Gifts and have *basil-scented farts*

OR

have *butter-soaked skin, a maple scone for a foot,* get 5 o'clock *shadow all over your body,* have a *vast coaster* collection, have *Carl Weathers* borrow your pen and never *give it back,* and have *a bulimia that causes you to want to throw* up in mail *slots?*

YOU MUST CHOOSE!

Would you rather...

sneeze the sound of thunder

OR

pee pure energy?

YOU MUST CHOOSE!

CHAPTER SIXTEEN

SEXUALLY EXTREME

Because one sex chapter wouldn't be extreme enough...

If your life depended on it, would you rather have to have sex to the point of orgasm...

while staying on a running treadmill **OR** staying on a unicycle without falling off?

on a pogo stick **OR** on a seesaw without either end hitting the ground?

on an exercise ball without falling off **OR** sitting on a George Foreman Grill enduring the pain?

Would you rather...

have bland unspectacular sex with Antonio Banderas
OR
wild, passionate, freaky sex with Greg Gumbel?

YOU MUST CHOOSE!

Would you rather...

have bland unspectacular sex with Jessica Biel

OR

wild, passionate, freaky sex with Condoleezza Rice?

Would you rather be seduced by...

food **OR** music?

poetry **OR** massage?

origami **OR** shadow puppets?

Would you rather...

when getting too into it during sex, "tilt" like a pinball machine and stop functioning for a while

OR

be transported to Des Moines every time you orgasm?

YOU MUST CHOOSE!

355

Would you rather...

have to wear noise-proof headphones during sex

OR

a full leg cast?

Would you rather...

have sex with someone with problem flatulence

OR

with someone who has a life-size portrait tattoo of your uncle on their back?

Would you rather...

have to talk during sex in baby talk

OR

in beatnik slang from the '60s?

YOU MUST CHOOSE!

Would you rather...

have sex with Abu from *Aladdin*

OR

Flounder from the *Little Mermaid*?

Would you rather...

have a variety of conjunctivitis of the eye which, during sex, causes your partner to intermittently appear as Mao Tse Tung

OR

have to conduct all sexual activity in a pile of mulch?

Would you rather...

have a *Star Trek*–themed wedding **OR** a *Batman*–themed one?

an *Ewok*–themed wedding **OR** an *A-Team*–themed one?

a robot–themed wedding **OR** a Paul Bunyan–themed one?

YOU MUST CHOOSE!

Would you rather...

have your Facebook status update automatically report all specific sexual activity as you partake to the last detail

OR

have your Facebook profile display a complete group of people you've hooked up with?

Would you rather...

only be able to sleep with your best friend's sloppy seconds

OR

have to get your mother's written approval before sleeping with anyone?

Would you rather...

have a threesome with Colin Farrell and Artie Lang

OR

Matt Lauer and Bob Sagat?

YOU MUST CHOOSE!

Would you rather...

have a threesome with Gisele Bündchen and Rosie O'Donnell

OR

with two average looking women?

Would you rather...

have sex in an airplane bathroom

OR

on a golf course at night?

Would you rather...

have a magic screensaver that anticipates when someone
is coming into the room and automatically closes pornography

OR

a magic screensaver that shows you whatever Charlie Rose
is doing at the time?

YOU MUST CHOOSE!

SEXUALLY EXTREME

Would you rather...

have your mom look at your current Internet browsing history

OR

at all of your last month's emails to your significant other?

Would you rather only be able to have sex...

missionary **OR** doggie-style?

oral sex **OR** intercourse?

performing a 69 **OR** 37?

Would you rather...

tell your partner everything about your sexual past

OR

tell them every sexual thought you have about another person?

YOU MUST CHOOSE!

Would you rather use as a sex toy...

a menorah **OR** a slab of beef?

a backscratcher **OR** a Rubik's Snake?

a Wacky WallWalker **OR** a double cheeseburger?

You live with a roommate. You decide to use a blacklight to reveal hidden "stains."

Would you rather...

find stains all over your coffee mug

OR

all over a picture of you and your family?

YOU MUST CHOOSE!

Would you rather...

speak like a pirate during sex

OR

yodel upon orgasm?

Things to consider: asking to have your timbers shivered

Would you rather...

be a supervillain that can kill people's sex drive at any moment
with the perfect personalized mood-killing hologram

OR

a supervillain who can queef 4.5 richter scale earthquakes?

Would you rather...

have orgasms that feel like doing a whippet

OR

that feel like jumping into the ocean on a hot day?

YOU MUST CHOOSE!

Would you rather...

have sex with Pinocchio

OR

with your choice of *Snow White* dwarf?

If your life depended on it, would you rather...

have to bring yourself to orgasm while your mom leaves you a long rambling answering machine message

OR

while staring, eyelids held open, at a poster of an adorable kitten?

Would you rather...

have porn quality sex but porn quality conversation as well

OR

have romantic comedy quality sex and romantic comedy quality conversation?

YOU MUST CHOOSE!

THREE-WAYS WITH CELEBRITY SUPERCOUPLE FISH

Would you rather have a three-way with...

Albacore (Jessica Alba and Corey Feldman) **OR** Katfish (Kat Von D and Laurence Fishburne)?

Sardean (Sarah Michelle Geller and Dean Cain) **OR** Halibut (Halle Berry and Boutros Boutros-Ghali — alternative name Boutros Boutros Halle)?

Moray (Demi Moore and Ray Liotta) **OR** Portmanteau (Natalie Portman and Tony Danza)?

YOU MUST CHOOSE!

Would you rather...

watch your parents having sex

OR

watch your grandparents having sex?

Would you rather...

be unable to shake the sporadic image of Gene Shalit during sexual congress

OR

have pubic hair that grows whenever you're lying?

Would you rather...

have asparagus for nipples

OR

have a unique venereal disease where anytime you kiss someone you briefly turn into an 1800s gold prospector, who is dead-set on the finding that next big strike?

YOU MUST CHOOSE!

Would you rather...

be unable to perform sexually unless dressed up as a Spanish conquistador

OR

when attempting to shout out your partner's name when having sex, always instead yell "Stombin 6!"?

Would you rather...

have to wear foam "Number 1" hands when having sex

OR

have to wear loafers without socks?

Would you rather...

have sex with Yao Ming

OR

Orville Redenbacher?

YOU MUST CHOOSE!

Would you rather...

have genitalia that permanently reduces in size five percent each time it is used

OR

genitalia that multiplies after fifty uses?

Would you rather...

have your libido vary directly with the stock market

OR

have the sexual outcome of your dates be contingent on what base you reach, if any, via a roll of dice in Strat-O-Matic baseball?

Would you rather...

have one of your sexual encounters webcast

OR

appear in a Zagat-style guide based on submissions from your various sexual partners?

Things to consider: a "bumbling novice" who "couldn't find a clitoris with a divining rod" offers "mildly pleasant groping" and is "over in a flash."

YOU MUST CHOOSE!

367

PICK YOUR PENIS

Would you rather...

have a penis that beeped like a Geiger counter the closer you get to a partner willing to put out

OR

have a penis that dispensed freshly brewed coffee?

Would you rather...

have a penis the consistency of bamboo

OR

the consistency of one of those water-filled things—I think it was called a snake—y'know, that rubber thing... you'd like squeeze it, and it'd squirm, that thing! From the eighties, you know what I'm talking about?

YOU MUST CHOOSE!

Would you rather...

have a clitoris that doubled as the on/off button for your television

OR

have a "mood clitoris" that changed color depending on your emotional state?

Would you rather...

only be able to sleep with sexual partners over the height of 7' **OR** under the height of 4'?

partners weighing over 500 lbs **OR** under 70 lbs?

partners whose names have exactly 11 letters **OR** partners born in Wyoming?

Would you rather...

walk in on your mother delivering a BJ to Terrence Trent D'Arby

OR

walk in on your father masturbating to images of Chef Boyardee?

YOU MUST CHOOSE!

Would you...

dunk your scrotal sack in a pot of boiling water for ten seconds for $50,000?

Would you rather...

only be able to get turned on when your partner is dressed like Thurgood Marshall

OR

by listening to Shaquille O'Neal's album *Shaq-Fu: Da Return*?

Would you rather...

be completely incapable of moving when sexually attracted to someone

OR

mentally revert to yourself as 4 year-old whenever you are about to have any sort of sexual contact?

YOU MUST CHOOSE!

During sex, would you rather your partner say...

"I love you!" **OR** "F**k me!"?

"You're the greatest!" **OR** "Give it to me!"?

"Eisenhower shall return!" **OR** "The overlord shall be pleased!"?

Would you rather...

give birth to a baby with fully developed private parts
OR
with wings instead of arms?

Would you rather...

have your dirty talk dubbed with clean sound-alike words
(eg. "Fork that pony!"; "Sick that dog!")
OR
ejaculate Clearasil?

YOU MUST CHOOSE!

Would you rather have...

phone sex **OR** cybersex?

Telegraph sex **OR** Pictionary sex?

Morse code sex **OR** snail mail sex?

Would you rather...

be the world's greatest lover but marry your high school sweetheart at age 18

OR

have the talents of Shakespeare but be restricted to writing for *Penthouse Forum*?

Would you rather...

like big butts and be unable to fabricate about such matters

OR

find out your girlfriend is a centerfold, causing your blood temperature to starkly plummet?

YOU MUST CHOOSE!

Would you rather...
have sex with Kathy Griffin

OR
with Jessica Simpson in a bed of rusty nails?

Would you rather...
have a commemorative chess set made from your various sexual partners

OR
have Ken Burns make a nine part documentary about your sex life?

Would you rather...
always be drunk during sex

OR
never be drunk during sex?

YOU MUST CHOOSE!

Would you rather...

have sex on bed sheets depicting bloody scenes from wars

OR

sheets with smiling pictures of your parents?

Would you rather...

have to list your penis size/breast size on your business card

OR

have to use the email for all business and pleasure: hobbitpumper@gmail.com?

Would you rather...

use a Netflix system for condoms

OR

toilet paper?

YOU MUST CHOOSE!

Would you rather...

have a penis of ever-changing girth

OR

have balls of ever-changing weight?

Would you rather...

have an ass crack that is 2/3 the way to the left of your body

OR

have an ass crack that extends up to and between your shoulder blades?

Would you rather...

only be able to communicate during romance and sex through facial expression

OR

text message?

YOU MUST CHOOSE!

CHAPTER SEVENTEEN

EXTRA EXTREMELY EXTREME

Now we are talking. Even yelling a bit. We have traversed the realm of the slightly extreme, skipped right over the somewhat extreme into the dangerous territory of the fairly extreme. And now we find ourselves in the terrifying, tantalizing, titillating redundant world of the Extra Extremely Extreme. Put on your safety vest and special person's pads, and get ready to push it … to the extremely extreme! Extra-ly!

Would you rather live in a world where...

babies had mute buttons

OR

where parents did?

Would you rather...

belch the scent of roses

OR

fart smooth jazz?

Would you rather...

be eating a burrito and discover a long, long hair in your mouth

OR

be licking a Tootsie Pop, only to find a small human embryo in the middle?

YOU MUST CHOOSE!

Would you rather...

have a voice whose volume is permanently set at the equivalent of 8 on a stereo

OR

speak at ten times normal speed?
Things to consider: child-rearing, sex

Would you rather...

sleep nightly in pajamas made of dentists' used gauze

OR

have to reach into a horse's ass every time you want the key to your apartment?

Would you rather...

have a ballet based on your life

OR

have a melodramatic cheesy *90210*-like show based on your life?

YOU MUST CHOOSE!

Would you rather watch...

"The Mormon Bachelor"

30 hopeful beautiful single ladies compete, but only three to five will be chosen to be the wives of the... *The Mormon Bachelor*. Consider the intrigue when the Mormon Bachelor finds a girl he really likes but she doesn't get along with the other prospective spouses, threatening the cohesiveness of the unit.

OR

"Foreign or Retarded" (game show)?

Would you rather...

breathe to the tune of "Mr. Roboto"

OR

have your speech badly dubbed over like in a Japanese monster movie?

Would you rather...

be a Siamese octuplet

OR

have to raise octuplets?

Things to consider: hoping to be a "corner unit" in the octuplet chain, playing Red Rover

YOU MUST CHOOSE!

Would you rather live in a world where...

it is illegal for people under 18 to buy cigarettes

OR

where it is illegal for people over 40 to buy cigarettes?

Things to consider: Cigarette smoking starts to seriously affect your health if you smoke after 40, whereas smoking up to that point has little statistical effect on health. Why the hell do we ban them for young people when it would make a lot more sense in terms of social cost and societal health to ban smoking for older adults? Next caller.

Would you rather...

have genital warts

OR

eyeball zits?

Would you rather... (Jewish moms only)

have your daughter date a gentile man

OR

a Jewish woman?

YOU MUST CHOOSE!

381

Would you rather...

DROOL DRAIN-O

EXHALE RAID?

Would you rather...

be twisted like a balloon animal

OR

be a human puck on a giant air hockey table of the gods?

Things to consider: How long it would take for you to die and how would it happen?

Would you rather...

only be able to eat garnish to survive

OR

only be able to drink human-lactated milk?

Would you rather...

have your fingernails peeled off, one by one

OR

your hair, head and body, pulled out one by one?

Would you rather...

speak like Martin Luther King with a horrible lisp

OR

like Johnny Carson in the middle of taking a dump?

YOU MUST CHOOSE!

WOULD YOU RATHER...? HOBO TRAITS

Would you rather...

carry all your personals including a laptop in a hobo bag on a stick

OR

only be able to travel by freight train cars?

Would you rather...

have all kinds of crazy stunts happen to you like Charlie Chaplin's the *Little Tramp*

OR

not?

Would you rather...

have hobo charcoal marks on your face

OR

have a dreadful PTSD alcoholic, homeless lifestyle that is inaccurately romanticized by movies and popular culture?

YOU MUST CHOOSE!

Would you rather...

occasionally "lose reception" in face to face dialogue and be unable to hear what people are saying

OR

be compelled to dance like a stripper whenever you see a pole of any kind?

Would you rather...

have to keep a hard-boiled egg in your mouth at all times

OR

have to keep one in your ass at all times?

Would you rather live in...

a massive house of cards **OR** a house of mirrors?

a house of glass **OR** wicker?

a house of Nerf **OR** chocolate?

YOU MUST CHOOSE!

Would you rather...

grate all of your back skin off

OR

microwave your head for ten seconds?

Would you rather...

have to type forever with no vowels

OR

no hands?

Would you rather...

be able to decipher the handwriting of any doctor

OR

be able to generate angst in turtles?

YOU MUST CHOOSE!

Would you rather...

(pirates only) never be able to say "Aarrgh"

OR

have a sissy pink sequined eye patch?

Would you rather...

use gasoline as shampoo

OR

wipe yourself with extra-adhesive tape?

Would you rather...

have foldable Swiss army knife devices for fingernails

OR

have nunchucks for hair?

YOU MUST CHOOSE!

Would you rather go on a trip to...

Striking Baseball Fantasy Camp—Make lavish demands with real big leaguers! Sleep til noon and attend dive-bars and get drunk! These are just a few of the tantalizing childhood fantasies you can live out when you get to hang out with baseball players doing what they do best—striking!

OR

Vietnam War Reenactment Weekend—Relive history! Simulate jungle warfare, ingest Agent Orange, flip out and burn an innocent village to the ground, and shoot your own troops. Fun and educational!

Would you rather...

only be able to have sex on Tuesdays

OR

only during even minutes of the day (3:22, 3:24, 3:26, etc.)?

Would you rather...

be a chronic procrastinator

OR

(work in progress)?

YOU MUST CHOOSE!

Would you rather...

go shoe shopping with Larry

OR

tell Renaldo he is overreacting?
Things to consider: Larry's deliberation, Renaldo's temper

Would you rather...

have cow-sized nipples

OR

have all your dirty words and vulgar expressions censored with silly bleeps, buzzes, and cuckoos?

Would you rather...

have to walk with your feet never leaving the ground

OR

never be able to use the same word twice in any given 24-hour period?
Things to consider: Try both for a day.

YOU MUST CHOOSE!

EXTRA EXTREAMELY EXTREME

Would you rather live in a world where...

scratching your crotch prevented cancer

OR

where the mythic figures of childhood fantasy were real? (i.e., the Tooth Fairy, Easter Bunny, Santa Clause, the Lord of Brisket.)

Would you rather...

have the hands of a 90 year-old

OR

the boobs of a 90 year-old?

Would you rather...

use your mouth to change a light bulb

OR

to flush a public toilet?

YOU MUST CHOOSE!

Would you rather play...

Fantasy Basketball - White Edition

Players choose exclusively white players from the NBA and score points for picks set, hustle baskets, scrapping for loose balls, "doing the intangibles", smart, heady play, unselfishness, moving well without the ball, etc.

OR

Magnetic Militant Black Poetry

Boasts magnetic tabs on which you'll find words like, "whitey", "die", "the Man", and "oppression". Sample poem: "the Man burns. Whitey Oppression." 300 magnetic tabs.

Would you rather...

only be able to use thermometers rectally

OR

be able to use thermometers by mouth but only ones that have been previously used rectally (you can rinse them)?

YOU MUST CHOOSE!

Would you rather...

BE A SIAMESE TWIN WITH YAO MING

OR

MINI-ME?

Would you rather...

only be able to sleep in trees **OR** under cars?

in airports **OR** hanging upside down like a bat?

at rock concerts **OR** on crabbing boats?

Would you rather...

pierce your cheek **OR** your knee?

your tongue **OR** your fingertip?

your uvula **OR** your perineum?

Would you rather...

have glow in the dark acne

OR

have caramel ear wax?

YOU MUST CHOOSE!

Would you rather...

have a chauffeur who is an insecure 15 year-old getting his learner's permit

OR

a chauffeur who is a 90 year-old grandmother?

Would you rather...

have to clean yourself like a cat

OR

take a dump in a box of litter like a cat?

Would you rather...

be a Siamese twin connected by the nose

OR

by the buttcheeks?

YOU MUST CHOOSE!

Would you rather...

communicate in the tone of a sappy Hallmark card

OR

in Def Comedy?

Would you rather...

hammer a nail through your hand

OR

use boiling water eye drops?

Would you rather...

defecate colorful and intricate kaleidoscope patterns

OR

urinate in solid rods?

YOU MUST CHOOSE!

Would you rather...

have to use an Amish hospital

OR

have your only source of education be the back of oatmeal packets?

Would you rather...

snore the sound of a trumpet

OR

with the power of a vacuum?

Would you rather...

have your bedroom designed like a prison cell

OR

like a giant version of a hamster cage?

Things to consider: cedar chips, exercise wheel

YOU MUST CHOOSE!

Would you rather...

do this connect the dots **OR** this one?

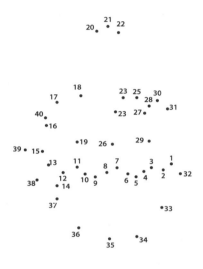

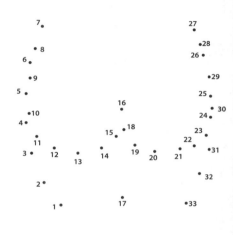

YOU MUST CHOOSE!

Would you rather...

be constantly followed by an environmentalist who loudly points out everything you do that's killing the environment

OR

be followed around by a personal trainer who loudly points out everything you do that's bad for yourself?

Would you rather...

have ears that face backwards

OR

eyes that blink sideways?

Would you rather...

date an otherwise hot person with bad cauliflower ear

OR

terrible turkey neck?

YOU MUST CHOOSE!

Would you rather...

have your rectum located in the palm of your hand

OR

on the bottom of your foot?

Would you rather...

have your heart located outside your chest

OR

have your skin and flesh stop short of your feet like Capri pants?

Would you rather...

be able to dispense salt and pepper out of your nostrils

OR

be able to fill in bubbles on multiple choice tests with enviable precision?

Would you rather...

be a dew drop on a tulip

OR

be a tear drop of joy?

YOU MUST CHOOSE!

Would you rather...

have a retractable ball-point pen in your finger

OR

have a laser pointer finger?

Would you rather...

have a sleep disorder that causes you to appear as Joey Ramone any time you lie down

OR

not be able to remember every other minute of your life?

Would you rather...

breathe through your navel

OR

your butt?

Things to consider: snorkeling

YOU MUST CHOOSE!

Would you rather...

get caught in a snowstorm of throwing stars

OR

a rainstorm of sulfuric acid?

Would you rather...

have sex with a 50% scale Brad Pitt

OR

a regular-sized Bob Costas?

Would you rather...

have sex with a 200% scale Shakira

OR

Kate Winslet?

YOU MUST CHOOSE!

401

Would you rather...

wear a three-cornered hat

OR

wear reverse heels where the toe is six inches higher than the heel?

Would you rather...

have a Nerf lawn

OR

have bean-bag bushes?

Would you rather...

purposely run over a squirrel

OR

slap a full-nelson on an elderly stranger for five minutes?

Would you rather...

have moving tattoos

OR

a tattoo that changed each day to an image that expressed how you are feeling?

YOU MUST CHOOSE!

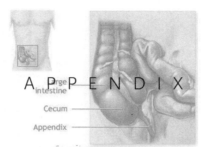

Large
intestine

Cecum

Appendix

APPENDIX

ROADKILL:
ADDITIONAL TRAVEL GAMES

ROADKILL CAR BINGO

Divide into two teams. Each team picks a Bingo page.
Each time you spot one of the items below, mark the box.

Person giving the finger	Someone singing to themselves in a car	Drunk person on street
Jaywalker	Doobie Brothers song on radio	Nose-picker
Asshole who cuts you off	Religious zealot bumper sticker	Roadkill—deer, fox, or pelican

Card 1

The first team to mark three boxes in a row, horizontally, vertically, or diagonally wins. Or if you're not into the whole competition thing, work together.

Card 2 (If necessary, tear this page out. Take it to the Man!)

Obese person eating in car	Graffiti with a misspelling	Audible fart
Mustard	Guy driving who thinks he is cooler than he actually is	Fuzzy Dice
Vanity license plate with sexual content	Guilt	Roadkill—squirrel, possum, or Ewok

ROADKILL SNAP JUDGMENT

Look at a car ahead of you. Guess what the person will look like based on their car. Include race, age, and sex. Be specific. For example, if you see a Volvo up ahead, you might say, "a middle-aged mom who's lost any sense of her sexuality", while another passenger might say "a hipster with horn-rimmed glasses." If you see a low-rider, you could guess "a bad-ass vato gang member" or "a redneck teenager smoking." Speed up (safely), get next to the car and look (safely) and see who is closest. Repeat (safely). First one to five points wins (safely).

Authors are not responsible for bad or irresponsible driving.

BATTLE HAIKU ROADKILL

Here's how this works: Two people engage in Battle
Haiku, where they insult each other à la Battle Rap.
But instead of rap, use the lost art of Japanese Haiku
poetry. The poems must insult the opponent in a good-
natured way and follow a syllable pattern of 5-7-5.
Invoking nature is encouraged. Examples follow.

You have ugly teeth
Smile looks like wilting lotus
Crapped on by hawk

Well, you are so fat
Flesh is like cumulus cloud
Drifting in the wind.

Damn, yo!

ROADKILL

FACE OFF

Whoever is reading must convey the words below using charades. But here's the catch. You can only use your body from the neck up (i.e., your face).

- Disgusting
- Cross-eyed
- Drunk
- Horny
- Cunnilingus
- Pink Eye
- William H. Macy
- Supercilious

Team 1

See how many you can get in three minutes. If you'd like, split into teams. Each time you use a part of your body other than your face, deduct one point. Winner gets the next food stop paid for.

Team 2

- Excited
- Death
- Worry
- Gum
- Sexy
- Spit
- Vomit
- Vasco da Gama

ROADKILL TWO TRUTHS AND A LIE

Each person shares 3 one- or two-sentence stories about themselves, two of which are true. The, the others guess which is the lie.

Here's an example from the authors.

- A model dating a seven-footer was impressed with the use of seven-footers in our books and set Gomberg up on a date with another model.

- Two friends solicited Heimberg via email and he made a tour to "visit" each of them. They asked that they someday be mentioned in one of the books.

- Gomberg hooked up with a professional Cyndi Lauper look-alike.

To find our which is a lie, email:
twotruthsonelie@sevenfooter.com

BELOW THE BELT

Whoever is reading must convey the words below using charades. But her's the catch. You can only use your body from the waist down. (Driver, keep your eyes on the road!)

- Baseball
- Pray
- Ejaculate
- Shake
- Athlete's Foot

- Poop
- Rocket
- Crabs
- Pendulum
- Croissant

Don't stop there. Have someone choose more words and whisper them to the actor.

ROADKILL MIND CONTROL

Each player or team reads an Objectives Page (and does not look at the other Objectives Page). Read the objectives to yourself, making sure that no one else sees them. Now, go about your business as you normally would, looking for opportunities to achieve your objectives.

MIND CONTROL OBJECTIVES PAGE 1

Get an opponent to:

- Retrieve an item from the garbage.
- Draw the "Peace" symbol.
- Unbutton a button on another person's clothing.
- Say "radish" and "milk" in the same sentence.
- Say "nice shot."
- Put on another person's glasses.
- Imitate a farm animal.

All of the objectives require you to get one of your opponents to do something. It can be any one of your opponents, and not all opponents must be present when the objective is achieved. After you successfully achieve an objective and verbally reveal it to your opponent(s), reward yourself one point. The game is over when a player successfully scores three points.

MIND CONTROL OBJECTIVES PAGE 2

Get an opponent to:

- Say "You're/You are an idiot."

- Give the "thumbs-down" sign.

- Sing a line from a Beatles song.

- Perform a push-up.

- Say "plum" and "asparagus" in the same sentence.

- Put his/her own finger in his/her own ear.

- Clap.

About the Authors

Justin Heimberg is the author of all kinds of comedy books for all ages including the best-selling *Would You Rather...?* series (over 650,000 books in print). He is a professional screenwriter who has worked with studios such as Disney, Paramount, and Universal and collaborated with talent such as Jerry Bruckheimer and Jason Alexander. Justin has served as a humor writer/contributing editor for magazines including *Details, Esquire,* and *MAD.* With David Gomberg, Justin runs Seven Footer Entertainment, an entertainment company specializing in short and funny creative projects and services. A trained improvisational performer, Justin is the creator of the Award-winning *Documentary* at Improv Olympic. He lives in the Washington D.C. area. Justinheimberg.com.

David Gomberg is an outsider from planets dominated by evil forces. He resembles a furless monkey crossed with a sickly dog, and has a vaguely human-like face. He is grey in color, with the slightest hints of violet. For no apparent reason, his shoulders jut sharply up in ugly extremeties. Growing along his back and from his front legs, are sharp quills. Gomberg spends the time when he isn't hunting, howling. The eerie, resonating noise causes anyone who hears it for an extensive amount of time to go mad. When hunting, Gomberg travels in packs. He attacks prey by charging in, then leaving again, then charging back, and so on. He causes damage in this method by thrashing about and scratching prey with his sharp quills. Occasionally, Gomberg might also bellow a particularly focused howl in the victim's face. Gomberg, strangely, is sometimes valued and trained as a mounted steed.

If you wish to contact the authors, email authors@sevenfooter.com.